Contents

Introduction

We proclaim Jesus Christ and promote communities of joy, hope, love, and peace.[1] —World Church Mission Statement

This mission statement flows easily, but it is much more than a simple phrase. It is the plumbline by which we should evaluate all the projects we are considering and all the investments of time, energy, and resources—both individually and collectively.

We will become a worldwide church dedicated to the pursuit of peace, reconciliation, and healing of the spirit.[2] —Transforming Goal

In June 1997, President W. Grant McMurray challenged the church with this goal as the contemporary expression of the church's mission. World Conference 2000 offered an opportunity to celebrate all that we have accomplished and to accept the challenges of the future. Conference action (WCR 1268) adopted a name that better describes what the church is attempting to be—Community of Christ. Our new name articulates in a new and clear way what has always been our call and our identity: We are a people called to witness of Jesus Christ and to promote communities that embody Christ's shalom. In the midst of our celebration and acceptance of change, we were reminded that we are at a beginning, not an end, of our journey of transformation. *"The road to transformation is the path of the disciple"* (Doctrine and Covenants 161:3d). We are called to the future—a commitment to walk the path of the disciple.

Theme Scripture

From that time Jesus began to proclaim, "Repent, for the kingdom of heaven has come near." As he walked by the Sea of Galilee, he saw two brothers, Simon, who is called Peter, and Andrew his brother, casting a net into the sea—for they were fishermen. And he said to them, "Follow me, and I will make you fish for people." Immediately they left their nets and followed him.

As he went from there, he saw two other brothers, James son of Zebedee and his brother John, in the boat with their father Zebedee, mending their nets, and he called them. Immediately they left the boat and their father, and followed him.
                                                                    —Matthew 4:17–22

A Call to Discipleship—Grant McMurray[3]

[In each chapter, the section titled "A Call to Discipleship" will contain an excerpt from the World Conference address delivered by Grant McMurray on April 3, 2000. The full text of this sermon is reproduced in the appendix.]

It is a daunting task to stand at the bridge to a new millennium and speak about the future of the church I love. To speak truth to such a moment is to lay down the barriers of conventionality and be willing to press against the boundaries of possibility. To speak truth to such a moment is to be willing to both embrace the incredible energy and excitement of our gathering and what we have accomplished together and at the same time to proclaim soberly that it is not enough, that the future demands something from us that is deeper, more risky, more challenging than any celebration will allow.

[During Transformation 2000 we] embraced change, not begrudgingly but enthusiastically, arguing that we must be transformed if we are to fulfill our mission. At the same time, we embraced our story and declared that indeed we are different and we do have something unique to contribute. In the process we recast that story so as to discover the mythic truths that lay shimmering at its core. From out of persecution and rejection we discovered peace and reconciliation. From out of exclusive, gathered American communitarian experiments we discovered inclusive global community. From out of a ritualistic temple cultus we discovered an expansive, symbolic, and sacramental understanding of temple theology. . . .

[We] summon the church to a transforming faith that moves us prophetically into the future, not knowing where our journey might take us, but assured that we are led by the God who birthed this people on the frontier and now leads us toward the peaceable kingdom, which we call Zion. We are called to be disciples, to follow Jesus Christ. It is he who makes for peace, who reconciles, and heals…. But now we are asked to go deeper, to go beyond the words that touch the imagination so as to encounter the Spirit, which compels the response. It is to take the sometimes long pathway from the mind to the heart, connecting the two in an unbroken thread of knowing and doing. It is to lay aside predispositions and tired bromides that soothe but do not inspire, and instead to take up the cross and walk the path of the disciple.

1. Ask class members to review the six disciplines as given in Appendix B. During their personal meditation or study time, encourage them to create additional images and language that illustrate unity and distinctiveness. This is an exercise that can stimulate the imagination and allow for the use of metaphors, similes, and poetic language that will help in the exploration of the path of discipleship.

2. Read Doctrine and Covenants Section 161 together. (See Appendix A.) What topics emerge that the class would like to discuss? Make a list on a flip chart (or chalkboard). As the class meets in future sessions, be sure to address these topics as well as the class material.

Where We Must Go

There is a wonderful story from Africa. Missionaries needed to make their way from one village to another through the heart of a deep and forbidding jungle. They inquired about the best possible guide to lead them on their dangerous journey. They had been warned that the path through the jungle was hard to discern, and without the proper guide they would surely lose sight of the path. They finally found a person who they were assured knew the correct path through the jungle and could guide them safely to where they needed to be. As they started through the thick jungle, they could not see the path ahead of them as they moved. They became increasingly alarmed as the guide took them farther and farther into the jungle with no visible path ahead. Finally, they began to protest, "Where is the path? There is no path here. You are leading us into the deep jungle, and there is no path!" The guide looked calmly at the frightened followers and replied, "I am the path. It is me you follow."

So it is for us. Jesus *is* the path. The call to discipleship requires discipline and intentionality as we step out in faith. Let us explore together how we can live out discipleship individually and institutionally.

This text is intended to stimulate thinking and conversations on six particular disciplines. Rather than giving definitive answers, all are encouraged to participate in the discussion. Each of these disciplines is one that disciples will seek to engage in and pursue. All responses will require intentional commitment to specific courses of action. Each disciple and community will determine specifically those courses of action. But make no mistake—if people truly engage in each of these disciplines, they will be transformed.

So let us share stories, thoughts, scriptures. What follows are simply places to begin the exploration of what practicing these disciplines might mean in each life. It is not an easy walk—the journey will be arduous. But there is joy in a journey made with friends, so let us embark!

Chapter 1

Build Community

Key Scripture

Open your hearts and feel the yearnings of your brothers and sisters who are lonely, despised, fearful, neglected, unloved. Reach out in understanding, clasp their hands, and invite all to share in the blessings of community created in the name of the One who suffered on behalf of all.

Be patient with one another, for creating sacred community is arduous and even painful. But it is to loving community such as this that each is called. Be courageous and visionary, believing in the power of just a few vibrant witnesses to transform the world. Be assured that love will overcome the voices of fear, division, and deceit.

Stand firm in the name of the One you proclaim and create diverse communities of disciples and seekers, rejoicing in the continuing fulfillment of the call to this people to prophetically witness in the name of Jesus Christ.

Heed the urgent call to become a global family united in the name of the Christ, committed in love to one another, seeking the kingdom for which you yearn and to which you have always been summoned. That kingdom shall be a peaceable one and it shall be known as Zion.

—Doctrine and Covenants 161:3a, c, 6a–b

1. What are the blessings of community?
2. Choose phrases out of this scripture that give direction for what is necessary to build community.
3. Think about the congregations of the church. How are they similar and how are they diverse? What is required to create and support diverse communities?

9

A Call to Discipleship—Grant McMurray[4]

First, the path of the disciple calls us to community. The people who built a teeming city of followers on the banks of the Mississippi are now called to build a diverse community of disciples from the farthest corners of the world. We will be a community that invites and embraces all those desiring a home in the body of Christ, including male and female, young and old, rich and poor, and people of all races, cultures, and life experiences.

With the model of Jesus as friend, we will create environments of worship and communion that support the discovery and use of each person's innate gifts, that nourish each soul and develop within each person the skills and confidence to succeed in life and ministry. Our understanding of evangelism is centered in it being the means through which the love of God is shared with the world. When such witness is done faithfully the church will be blessed through the diversity of our body and the breadth of our ideas and experiences.

Do not assume that such a declaration, which sounds virtuous and true, is easily achieved or without sometimes painful implications. It means we embrace the lives of people we may not understand, including choices with which we may not agree. It means we peer behind the surface of each one of us, knowing that if we believe in a God who creates human life, that God resides in the soul of every one. Our belief in community is founded upon our sure knowledge that the God in me seeks the God in you and that it is when we have encountered that divine reality at the very center of our faith that we finally, truly, know one another.

4. Brainstorm and list in front of the class any words that come to mind when one hears the word "community."

5. What questions or thoughts come to mind when the topic of community comes up? What needs clarification?

6. How do evangelism and community relate to each other?

7. What are some of the difficulties of building community? In what ways is diversity both a gift and a challenge?

8. How important are people's innate gifts to the community? How does a community discover and use the gifts of people?

Scripture Study

And the Lord called his people Zion, because they were of one heart and one mind, and dwelt in righteousness; and there was no poor among them.
—Doctrine and Covenants 36:2h, i

9. What do you think it means to be "of one heart and one mind"? Name principles so basic or essential that belief in them allows people to live together peacefully despite what might otherwise be "serious" differences of opinion.

There is no longer Jew or Greek, there is no longer slave or free, there is no longer male and female; for all of you are one in Christ Jesus.
—Galatians 3:28

10. It is easy to apply the terms used in this passage to the specific categories named. Christians can "overlook" differences such as race or gender. Slaves are equal in God's sight to their masters. For a moment, assume that Paul was simply trying to use terms that would represent the most dramatic differences that could exist between people. Think of labels that, in personal experience, would most separate or differentiate one person from another. Victim and offender? Jew and Muslim? Clean, well dressed, well mannered and filthy, ragged, rude, offensive? Bright, charming, articulate, accomplished and seriously retarded, disabled, dependent?

11. What does discipleship require? How is it possible to make all welcome into one community?

Exploring Community

What does it mean to be called to community? Community does not just refer to a passive coming together of people. A neighborhood is not, just because of proximity in which people live, the kind of community to which one is called as Christ's disciple. Christ's community is a committed coming together. It is intentional; it requires something of each person. It is both a nurturing environment and a vehicle for accomplishing more.

Stages of Community-Making

In the book *The Different Drum: Community-Making and Peace,* M. Scott Peck described four stages of community-making.[5]

11

Groups working deliberately toward community will usually grow through these stages.

Pseudocommunity is the "faking it" phase. The key dynamic in this phase is that the group avoids conflict. Do not confuse this with there *being* no conflict. The conflict is there; it is simply not acknowledged or dealt with. In true community, however, conflict is acknowledged and resolved. In pseudocommunity, conflict is avoided. In the phase of pseudocommunity, basic differences that exist among its members are simply denied. Everyone pretends to agree. Listening to conversations in pseudocommunities, one hears a lot of generalities. People make many blanket statements. They do not move to levels of individual differences. Instead they stay at a superficial level where they can appear to agree.

Chaos is moving past that "surface" of sameness and allowing individual differences to be shown and seen. In this phase, the group's members are busily trying to heal and convert one another. They are no longer trying to hide differences; they are instead trying to obliterate them! There are, of course, times when fully developed communities struggle. The difference is that in the chaos phase, the struggle is not effective—it goes nowhere. In true community, in the midst of struggle, people feel an excitement because they are assured that they will, somehow through the process, arrive at a wonderful consensus. There is no such assurance in chaos. In chaos, the struggle feels hopeless. There is no excitement, and there is certainly no fun! But even in this painful phase, there is hope to be offered. At least people move past the life of pretending that there are no differences.

Emptiness is the next phase of community building that most are not anxious to enter. Emptiness is the truly hard part. It requires that people "empty" themselves of all the barriers they have built to true communication. Peck lists the most common of these barriers:

expectations and preconceptions,
prejudices,
ideology, theology, and solutions,
the need to heal, convert, fix, or solve, and
the need to control.

This is not an exhaustive list. Peck suggests that each person in the group will need to explore and "name" what it is they must empty from themselves in order to move on into community. It is in a very real sense a time of sacrifice. Members of the group must identify and "give up" anything that stands in the way of genuine communication.

But as people begin to share those things that stand in their way—their own brokenness—almost inevitably there will be attempts to block those expressions of pain. People feel discomfort, and discomfort acts as a barrier. Such emptying is not solely an individual process. Community is more than just the sum of the individuals who come together. Peck writes of "little deaths" in the individuals and of a "death" of the group as it had existed. In order to be transformed into true community, the old forms must pass away. He makes no claim that this is an easy process.

Community means arrival! But wait, it may not be so simple. Community maintenance is not easy either. There will be times when the community will fall back into an "earlier" phase. There may be times of pseudocommunity and the need to once again enter chaos and experience emptying in order to restore true community. This process is not easy; it is neverending. But there are rewards. "When I am with a group of human beings committed to hanging in there through both the agony and the joy of community, I have a dim sense that I am participating in a phenomenon for which there is only one word. I almost hesitate to use it. The word is 'glory.'"[6]

12. Look at the community of a congregation and see who is there and who is *not* there. Who is excluded? How do we exclude people from our community? What can be done to remove barriers?

13. Describe an experience of true community. Did the community go through stages such as those described by M. Scott Peck? How were difficulties worked through? What "maintenance" does the community need to do?

14. Compare M. Scott Peck's "emptiness" stage of community with the idea to *"Respect each life journey"* (Doctrine and Covenants 161:3b).

15. Make a list of attitudes and elements that are needed to build community. Then make a list of barriers to real community.

16. What is the importance of repentance and prayer in building community? What is the importance of education and learning in building community?

Anxiously Engaged—Ken Barrows[7]

The point that most clearly defines Christian disciples is a common interest in celebrating God's incarnational presence in the world. As witnesses specifically of the life and ministry of Jesus Christ, we are receivers throughout time of the presence of God's Spirit. We share this common interest, in part, because we have chosen to follow as disciples and have made a covenant to that end. Equally important, we share in community because we believe that God has called us into this relationship with each other.

Discipleship and calling both imply intentionality; they do not just happen. We are members of the body of Christ precisely because we have chosen to be, and we stay together for precisely the same reason. That is why the creation of this type of community is plain hard work; it is not for those of shallow commitment or superficial intent.

Involvement in this community requires that one cultivate a willingness to build relationships that are based on mutuality and respect and to keep building even when such relationships falter. It requires that we recognize and celebrate our interdependence in the midst of a world that increasingly fosters independence as normative. It takes willingness to be influenced by others and to not feel less because of it. It takes hope instead of blind optimism, courage instead of bravado. Such a community fosters a willingness to seek that which is not yet while at the same time valuing that which has gone before, and, perhaps most difficult of all, it takes a willingness to make space for those who are "other" from ourselves, that they might exist and flourish within our midst.

In a very real way, the type of community we seek emerges as a result of our common interest to be engaged in reconciliation, sharing, learning, spiritual growth, and justice. These processes define both the nature and the scope of our efforts to create genuine community. It is almost as if we discover community by focusing somewhere else. As we engage in and grapple with the processes associated with bringing about reconciliation, stewardship of life, learning, growing spiritually, and justice, we discover, in our peripheral vision, the community we desire.

God's power is most clearly felt as the power of creative influence. God respects our ability to choose. The language of the Book of Mormon resonates when it declares that God's Spirit "entices" people to do good things in the world (Moroni 7:11). The parable of the women placing yeast in the measure of flour until it was leavened bespeaks this same type of creative power (Matthew 13:33; Luke 13:20). These illustrations speak the language of **influence** in the world rather than **domination** over it. The only power we have that accurately reflects the image of God's power in our lives is our ability to influence others to *be* good, and to *do* good, in the world. It is out of the relationships that grow between people who are seeking to develop these attributes in their lives that the synergy necessary to create transformative community will emerge.

We have been instructed specifically to *"Let nothing separate you from each other and the work whereunto you have been called"* (Doctrine and Covenants 122:17b). I believe this principle is foundational to the type of community we are called to create. We need to become a people who will, quite frankly, let nothing separate us from each other. When we come to those points within our relationships where we begin to draw the battlelines of separation, we need to stop and remember that we are called to incarnate within our community a higher principle: We are to be a body made up of many and diverse members all acting in harmony with each other under the influence of God's Spirit. The very one who modeled Christian discipleship willingly made the ultimate sacrifice on the cross for those who were not. Being a disciple engaged in the processes out of which community emerges is not about "being right"; rather it is about acting, speaking, thinking, and being in ways that allow place

15

for others to exist wholly and completely in our midst in ways that are mutually beneficial.

17. Ken Barrows wrote, "Discipleship and calling both imply intentionality." What kind of decisions and intentional actions need to be made to become disciples responding to such a calling?

18. When have you seen individuals or groups live out the instruction to "Let nothing separate you from each other and the work"?

Harambe!—Robert P. Bruch[8]

I remember walking a dusty path between two villages in Machocus District in Kenya, East Africa, and meeting two young boys walking to school. Their steps left perfect footprints in the red clay dust, and I was reminded that humankind has walked this earth for centuries seeking a more abundant life. In that situation, the drought had destroyed any possibility of a harvest.

As I visited with village leaders I asked, "What will you do in the face of this drought?" They answered, "Starvation may come to our village, and starvation may come to our families, but we will not despair."

They immediately organized a harambe workday. Harambe is the Kiswahili term that means "Let us work (or pull) together." One hundred fifty people showed up on the hillside and a leader lined them up on the contour.

An old man began to sing a chant, and each individual began to dig with a crude shovel or scrape with their bare hands. In rhythm to the chant they lifted dirt, a handful at a time. They tramped it in with bare feet, forming a terrace that would catch every possible drop of rain to grow food for the future.

The first several chants were in Kiswahili. I asked the meaning of it, and the translator replied, "These are the times, we are the people."

That chant has been embedded forever in my mind. When I am confronted with difficult tasks, those words come back to challenge me.

19. In what situations of your life does "These are the times, we are the people" speak to you?

Le Chambon

Lest Innocent Blood Be Shed: The Story of the Village of Le Chambon and How Goodness Happened There[9] is the story of a small village in southern France and the miracle it embodied during the Nazi occupation of France during World War II.

The people of the village of Le Chambon saved thousands of Jews. There was no organization responsible for the shelter and salvation of refugees. There was only a small village of Christians striving, as individuals and as a congregation, to live according to the gospel. Two things appear to have been instrumental in bringing into being that community of salvation. First, the people of Le Chambon were Hugenots, Protestants who in their history had known persecution as a minority in Catholic France since the Reformation. The lives of their ancestors had been dependent upon people willing to break the law to save other human beings, and they had developed a tradition of ignoring French law when the law conflicted with their conscience. Second, their pastor André Trocmé shared with the leadership of the village the conviction that the Sermon on the Mount was for real people living on Earth. It was not some ethereal vision of what would be nice; it was a statement of what is both possible and necessary.

This book is filled with stories of community. Many tell of momentous courage or brazen discipleship.

> During the first moments after Theis and I left the boardinghouse of the Marions, we walked separately through the snowy mountain wind. Two or three times Theis staggered and almost fell. Even I, with my younger reflexes, slipped once or twice. But when he reached out and intertwined his right arm with my left, suddenly the warmth of his thin body and the firmness of our intertwined arms created a new being moving upon four firm legs. Now we were stable, even though the icy road was still there, and even though the broom were still swirling their long evergreen fingers. The world was still cold, confusing, and dangerous. But we were close to each other, parts of a new whole, and we felt suddenly surefooted.[10]

20. When have you glimpsed Zionic community? How often were these experiences of community in the midst of hard times?

21. Discuss why the worth of all persons is basic to genuine community.

22. The people of Le Chambon broke the law of the Nazi regime to save the lives of refugees. What principles should guide Christians who might consider breaking the law of the land in order to create a more just situation in a community?

Conclusion

To walk the path of the disciple is a call to community. In the past, President McMurray reminded us, "we built cities in a search to blend the sacred and secular in a spatial environment."[11] Are we truly open to finding and living the transformed vision of community that is our future?

Closing

Sing together "Companions on the Journey" from *Sing a New Song* (*NS* 7), and close with prayer focused on the call to community.

Chapter 2

Seek
Reconciliation

Key Scripture

Become a people of the Temple—those who see violence but proclaim peace, who feel conflict yet extend the hand of reconciliation, who encounter broken spirits and find pathways for healing....

Do not be fearful of one another. Respect each life journey, even in its brokenness and uncertainty, for each person has walked alone at times. Be ready to listen and slow to criticize, lest judgments be unrighteous and unredemptive.

—Doctrine and Covenants 161:2a, 3b

1. Identify some of the conflicts that separate us from each other. Beside each one listed, put a word that you think is a more appropriate response rooted in the gospel.
2. How do we show that we "respect each life journey"?

A Call to Discipleship—Grant McMurray[12]

Second, the path of the disciple calls us to reconciliation. We have for too long allowed separations to define us. We cannot proclaim ourselves to be a people committed to reconciliation when we have festering sores of division within our own community. We will identify and seek to repair breaches in relationships within our body and with those who share our witness of the Restoration movement, but for reasons of doctrinal conflict or personal conflicts have separated from us.

I extend an open invitation to those of the Restoration

branches who are seeking a pathway to return. We desire to be reconciled. If we have hurt by our words or actions, we ask forgiveness. If we have been insufficiently patient or failed to understand, we will try to be better listeners. I extend the courtesies of my office, and those of other church leaders, to those who wish to dialogue with us about the ways we can share together from out of our common heritage. We pledge to be open, creative, and accepting and to seek every avenue of reconciliation.

We recognize that, in some cases, our differences over some issues may be such that we cannot return to full communion with each other. That does not indicate a failure to be reconciled if we are able to embrace one another in love, and extend God's blessing to each other, and share in such ways as may be satisfying. Judgments, characterizations, and attribution of unseemly motives are unworthy of our common callings to be disciples. Let us reason with one another, share the testimonies of our hearts, and be people of goodwill.

But our need to be reconciled extends beyond the boundaries of our own faith community. We have already begun and now must continue to overcome the things that separate us from other faiths and even from other religions of the world. Our commitment should be to coexist in love and peace, to be willing to learn from one another, to share our common witness to the extent we can, and to be respectful of those traditions that shape the souls of billions of people around the world.

To do so is not to divest ourselves of the zeal inherent in our own witness. It is to embrace the fundamental principle of the Christian, which is love of God and love of neighbor. For too long we have worried that exposure of our faith to those with differing beliefs somehow requires dilution of what we believe. To the contrary, a willingness to step forward aggressively into our communities, to sit at the table with priests and pastors, to engage in the interfaith discussions, is a way of proclaiming to the world who we are. We have things to say, contributions to make, a wonderful story worth recounting. Let us be reconciled to brothers and sisters of others faiths and religions by authentically expressing our witness and being respectful of theirs.

3. What are some of the "festering sores of division within our own community"? What steps would you suggest be taken to heal these sores? Where would you begin?

4. What attitudes are needed if we are to talk of reconciliation with another person or group who holds values or beliefs that are different from our own? What makes us uncomfortable with doing this? Is it necessary for either side to give up what they value in order to be reconciled?

5. Where does one begin when explaining identity and beliefs to another person or group?

Scripture Study

So if anyone is in Christ, there is a new creation: everything old has passed away; see, everything has become new! All this is from God, who reconciled us to himself through Christ, and has given us the ministry of reconciliation; that is, in Christ God was reconciling the world to himself, not counting their trespasses against them, and entrusting the message of reconciliation to us.

—II Corinthians 5:17–19

6. How is God calling you to become new? What must you give up in order to become new?

7. What might it mean that God has "given us the ministry of reconciliation"?

8. In what ways can we carry the message of reconciliation to others?

The Gospel of Matthew mentions often the need for reconciliation and for a respect of others' life journeys. The following are a few examples.

Blessed are the peacemakers, for they will be called children of God.

—Matthew 5:9

So when you are offering your gift at the altar, if you remember that your brother or sister has something against you, leave your gift there before the altar and go; first be reconciled to your brother or sister, and then come and offer your gift.

—Matthew 5:23–24

If another member of the church sins against you, go and point out the fault when the two of you are alone.

—Matthew 18:15

The Doctrine and Covenants also directs us to be reconciled to those who have offended us.

And if your brother or sister offend thee, thou shalt take him or her between him or her and thee alone.

—Doctrine and Covenants 42:23a

9. Read aloud the passages in either Matthew or Doctrine and Covenants 42, and list the prescribed method for addressing differences, which, though it begins privately, proceeds as needed through more public channels.

10. Read Section 161:3b about *"Respect each life journey"* and *"Be ready to listen and slow to criticize, lest judgments be unrighteous and unredemptive."* How do criticism and unrighteous judgment interfere with reconciliation and redemptive actions?

11. What should guide us in our determinations of when offenses really need to be taken to a more public forum? What can be done in some situations of hurt or offense to help involved parties see another perspective?

Exploring Reconciliation

Reconciliation is not only a matter of getting over the differences that separate us from our neighbors. For each of us, the discipline of reconciliation will impact our lives in many ways.

In a 1992 *Herald* article, President Emeritus Wallace B. Smith spoke of the need to be reconciled to history or heritage:

The need can be very real, whether we are talking about the need for reconciliation with our family heritage, our personal past, our understandings of our national history, our perceptions about church history, or any other aspect of history from which we feel alienated for whatever reason.[13]

Each individual must be reconciled with self and with one's personal past. Often there is some event or experience from the past that haunts us and prevents us from addressing what we need to do in the present. During a reunion, I [Anita Mortimer] found myself talking late into the night with a person about the pain of their marriage and divorce. Through sobs, this individual recounted to me unnerving stories of the abuse of self and children at the hand of the spouse. I had prosecuted

22

child abuse cases early in my career as an attorney, and my mind raced through the internal directory of agencies that could offer rescue from this intolerable suffering. But as I asked a few questions and processed the information I received in response, I realized that all these events had happened years ago. The children so graphically described as hiding in terror were now grown with families of their own. The marriage had ended decades ago. There had been no contact between these former spouses in years. Unable to reconcile with the past, this person continued to live within its terror and constraints. Twenty years of life had been sacrificed to a memory that lived on in the heart and mind of this person.

Reconciliation with one's past is not necessarily a simple thing. Some of us must overcome small hurdles in that process. Others have mountains to conquer. Victims of childhood trauma or abuse must often struggle with personal burdens in order to present whole selves in the service of God and neighbor. But reconciliation with past must be experienced in order to move forward freely and with full energy.

Just as we must reconcile ourselves with our personal past in order to give ourselves fully in service to God, some people are finding the need for reconciliation with the past of the church. We have heard our history in certain ways. As historians look objectively at the evidence from our collective past and share openly what they learn, some of us are hearing elements of our story that may not have been dealt with openly and can be confusing and create distrust or anger. We have to be willing to look at our history honestly, to move into good relationship with it, and let it be a positive force in future life and ministry.

Also we must be reconciled with one another. Reconciliation is not a one-time accomplishment. Anyone who has nurtured a long-term, successful friendship understands the ongoing nature of reconciliation. We have to keep at it. We have to constantly seek out the other and be honest and caring in our relationships. This is true not only within our particular faith community, but it is something we must be willing to exercise within our broader circle—individual with individual, faith community with faith community, and people with Earth's non-human nature—across all perceived borders that divide God's creations.

12. What actions can we take to reconcile our personal past? What can we do to help another experience reconciliation with their past? How does a community experience reconciliation with its past? Where can we go to learn more?

13. How can study and worship help us experience reconciliation?

14. At a meeting of a group called the Community of Concerned Citizens, an older gentleman entered and was greeted with smiles, waves, and "Hi, Chaplain." This was obviously a man who was held in high regard by the group. As the discussion of the inequities in the community between the people of the races continued, he spoke up. With anguish in his voice and tugging at his black skin, he cried, "Sometimes I hate this! I just wish I could walk out of my skin and be treated fairly." What kind of reconciliation is needed here?

15. Give some examples of reconciling with God's non-human creation.

A Disciple of Reconciliation—Darlene Caswell

Reconciliation ministries may be expressed in many ways. We see some examples of these in the life of one of the early disciples. The apostles gave Joseph, a Levite, the surname of Barnabas, meaning the *"son of encouragement"* (Acts 4:36). He is described as *"a good man, full of the Holy Spirit and of faith"* (Acts 11:24). In Acts 4:37 he is mentioned as having sold a field and then *"brought the money, and laid it at the apostles' feet."* Next he persuaded the apostles at Jerusalem to meet with Paul and hear his story (Acts 9:26–27). His presence at the time when Paul sought to unite with the early saints in Jerusalem was crucial to Paul's acceptance by that group and his ability to minister as a part of the early Christian church. In essence, Barnabas was saying, "Let's listen to Paul's story. Let's hear what he has been doing, and let's look at how his life has been changed. Let's give him a chance." Not only did he reconcile Paul with the apostles, he traveled with Paul to spread the gospel.

Undoubtedly Barnabas continued in the role of bridge

builder between the apostles and the church in Jerusalem on one side and Paul and the Gentiles on the other side. Many people believe the offering collected and taken by Barnabas and Paul to Jerusalem was partly based on the needs of the saints in Jerusalem and was partly an effort to express support and concern by the Gentile saints. This undoubtedly helped ease the tensions of the expanding church.

Barnabas invited a young man named John Mark to travel with them. Then something happened. John Mark left them at Cyprus. He must have felt a sense of failure and discouragement and may have dropped into a period of inactivity. But Barnabas saw in John Mark what he could become for the Lord and wanted him with them again. He wanted to give him a second chance. When Paul refused to have him, Barnabas saw that he could do the most by working with John Mark. Barnabas said goodbye to his friend Paul and traveled with John Mark. Because of this decision, John Mark again became actively involved in missionary work with the Gentiles. Many people believe that John Mark was the author of the Gospel of Mark. As a bridge builder and reconciler, Barnabas made it possible for the Christian church to benefit from the contributions of John Mark.

Barnabas, like so many, does not stand out among the greatest of those in the scriptures, but he served in a freeing, reconciling role. He encouraged others to use their gifts; he kept people talking to each other; he bridged differing ideas. He encouraged the discouraged and gave a second chance to those who had tried and failed. He opened doors, introduced, invited, stood by, and encouraged. By his example, we are called to do the same—to be agents of reconciliation and encouragement.

16. What do you suppose made it possible for Barnabas to be a reconciler?

17. Who are the people you know or have heard about who are reconcilers like Barnabas?

Reconciliation and the Dance of Being Female
—Mary Jacks Dynes[14]

In discussing reconciliation, I have to tell of my dance of being female—sharing who I am and where I have been. For too long I had been living out the script of the Silent Woman where stifling my truth took place.[15] In order to be a person of reconciliation, one must begin with oneself and be reconciled.[16]

A series of experiences and encountering a seemingly insignificant poster of Rembrandt's *Return of the Prodigal Son* (1668–1669) at a reconciliation retreat set in motion a long journey of looking back and pulling together what it means for me to dance the dance of being female in the Community of Christ and the wider church. This journey brought new reconciliation and understanding of my vocation (as a female) and offered me new strength.

I had already seen this painting of Rembrandt's prodigal son. It was larger than life with its abundant reds, browns, and yellows. Most of all, the light enveloped the embrace of the father and son surrounded by four mysterious bystanders. Clearly this was a "coming home," a time of deep reconciliation. But what most gripped me were the bystanders and most poignantly, the two women. I was struck by the woman in front, the one who was clearer and more distinct. She followed me throughout the room, and I could not look away from her. It wasn't her eyes that followed me throughout the room like the Mona Lisa (by Leonardo da Vinci) does in the Louvre Museum in Paris. It was her whole being that would not let me go. I was responding to something deep inside me, for this was a sacred moment. Here was a representation of where I was, at some distance and not sure I was a part of the whole homecoming scene. "[I]n a place much deeper than my head, I didn't feel included at all."[17]

Then, through an experience with the Divine, I saw that my power was to be compassionate love and empowerment for others. As a female, I thought in terms of circles and spirals rather than lines and levels, and I knew that relationships were very important to me. I tried to imagine a church in which it mattered less what someone's beliefs and practices were and more how relationships were nurtured and healed. I tried to imagine a church whose bottom line was relationship.

I came face to face with a system of social governance, a vast complex of patterns and attitudes within culture, religion, and family. The name of this system is patriarchy. But as Sue Monk Kidd pointed out, "It's important to emphasize that patriarchy is neither men nor the masculine principle; it is rather a system in which that principle has become distorted."[18] I had identified this patriarchy with the wider church and Carlo Carretto's words spoke to me:

> How baffling you are, oh Church, and yet how I love you! How you have made me suffer, and yet how much I owe you! I should like to see you destroyed, and yet I need your presence. You have given me so much scandal and yet you have made me understand sanctity. I have seen nothing in the world more devoted to obscurity, more compromised, more false, and I have touched nothing more pure, more generous, more beautiful. How often I have wanted to shut the doors of my soul in your face, and how often I have prayed to die in the safety of your arms. No, I cannot free myself from you, because I am you, although not completely. And where should I go?[19]

Part of this song that I must dance is the deep song of Christianity that lies beneath the patriarchal overlay. It's Christianity's inner life that includes the call to justice and compassion, meditation, the smell of bread and wine at the Communion table, and most importantly the life of Jesus. My song also questions the focus on suffering and the cross as central to redemption. Victimized suffering is not redemptive. What is redemptive is action that I take to extricate unjust suffering and how I can change the conditions that cause it.[20]

In addition this song that I dance to is one in which the use of language is very important, "[s]ince language not only expresses the world but helps to shape and create it."[21] So the core symbols we use for God become "the ultimate point of reference for understanding experience, life, and the world."[22] One can only imagine how the Divine feminine symbols will affect us as we answer the call to become a people of peace. What new ways of thinking, living, and acting will emerge and are emerging in our church when we integrate feminine symbols with other symbology?[23]

The song that I dance to also talks about the woman in back of Rembrandt's painting. You can just barely see her. Could she represent the women of color or women in developing countries? Are their voices being heard? How can they be empowered?

I will continue to dance my feminine dance with my granddaughters and with other women, helping them find their voices and connecting with them. I am still waking up, still healing, still reaching out to God for reconciliation, and still trying to come up with the courage to plant my heart in the world.[24]

18. What happens when people are expected to behave in a certain way and are not allowed to be themselves? How do they feel if they are not allowed to "be in the picture"?

19. Why is it that we get angriest with people and organizations that are closest to us?

20. Mary Jacks Dynes used the metaphor of the dance as she talked about reconciliation. Ask class members who are willing to strike a pose to demonstrate how the female dance would look—also the dance of ethnic groups, the poor, the male, the Christian. What does the dance of reconciliation look like?

Homecoming
Reflections on Rembrandt's *Return of the Prodigal Son*
—Danny A. Belrose[25]

And a woman is there—subtly, silently standing in the shadows.
A woman is there, undefined, shrouded in murky hues of muted
    light stripped of self, her smudged soul bleeding with the
    background.
Search carefully—"a woman is there,"
    unacknowledged, undesired, disconnected, peripheral.
    A woman is there—**just beyond the homecoming.**

A prodigal is there—recalcitrant, reclaimed, one shoe on, one
    shoe off
    dust discarded lost for gain of raced return.
Head bowed, kneeling, pregnant for welcome's healing word.
A prodigal is there—family, workers, friends, clustered so
    to celebrate the lost as found
    made sweet by father's long embrace.
But look once more—back behind the crowd

"a woman is there"—somewhere in the silence
hungering for a word, a touch, a wisp of warmth.
A woman is there—**just beyond the homecoming.**

A father's there—breathless down the path
    pursuing fractured faith—a child returned on wings of hope.
A mother's there—unrelenting, unforgetting, unyielding to the
    breech, joy's blinding tears confirming heartache's plea.
A brother's there—his torn response entwined with love and
    hate.
A ring, a robe, a fatted calf, the picture seems complete.
Not quite—There! There! Almost out of sight
    "a woman is there"—nameless in the night
    straining at the edges, fading from the scene.
    A woman is there—**just beyond the homecoming.**

A middle-aged man is there—unemployed, shattered home,
    tattered dreams.
A child is there—long hard nights, cold dark alleys,
    auctioned cheap to strange men in strange rooms.
An executive is there—Armani suits, sleek black cars,
    blue chip stocks and blue chip soul.
A lesbian is there—prisoner to self, screaming to get out,
    mute to family, friends and faith.
A four-year old battling leukemia, an elderly woman on Social
    Security, a teenage mother working two jobs...
Many faces, many races—
    not quite white enough, not quite tall enough, thin
    enough,smart enough.
Faceless faces translucent in the night, pushed to the edges
    not quite in the picture.
Look again! *There! There!* Can you see them?
They're all there—WAITING—**just beyond the homecoming.**

21. Which of the people in this poem do you identify with?
Why?

22. This poem by Danny A. Belrose speaks of the people on
the margins. It could easily have been used in the previous unit
about "community." How are the disciplines of community and

reconciliation connected? What ways must you practice both in order to live either?

Conclusion

To walk the path of the disciple calls us to reconciliation. "For reconciliation," McMurray stated, "we embraced the worth of persons, saying that all are called according to the gifts of God unto them."[26] How are we committed to valuing each person and the unique contribution they make to the body of Christ?

Closing

Sing together "Lord, Who Views All People Precious," *Hymns of the Saints (HS* 459), and close with prayer focused on the call to reconciliation.

Chapter 3

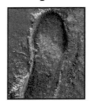

Share
Willingly

Key Scripture

Open your hearts and feel the yearnings of your brothers and sisters who are lonely, despised, fearful, neglected, unloved. Reach out in understanding, clasp their hands, and invite all to share in the blessings of community created in the name of the One who suffered on behalf of all.
—Doctrine and Covenants 161:3a

1. What are some of the yearnings you hear people talk about? What are your own yearnings?

A Call to Discipleship—Grant McMurray[27]

Third, the path of the disciple is to share willingly from the blessings of our lives. One of the cardinal principles of our faith is stewardship, but for too long we have shunted it off into its own box, left it to be interpreted by those with "temporal responsibilities," and wrongly assumed that it was about money and budgets…. [W]e join with the Presiding Bishopric in committing ourselves to a process of truly merging the function of the steward with the heart of the disciple.

Let's be blunt. Our people have been generous when challenged—witness the response to the building of the Temple and the call to support Transformation 2000. However, the overall interpretation of stewardship as we now understand it has increasingly lost the full support of several generations of church members. We continue to search for ways to define it so as to capture the imagination of each successive generation of stewards. We can no longer nod our head appreciatively about a principle, knowing all the while that many of us have not found a way to get it into our bone marrow. We *must* do something about it.

Our tithing filers and payers are the financial backbone of the church. In 1996 the Order of Evangelists invited me and my family to come to a reception in recognition of my ordination as president of the church. My mother, then eighty years old, came along. Brother [Everett] Graffeo provided my family members an opportunity to speak. He then asked Mom if she would like to say anything. Yeah, right, I thought. Like my soft-spoken, 5' 1" mother is going to stand up in front of this group and give a speech!

"Well, I believe I do have a few words to say," she said. The blood drained from my face. Oh no, what on earth is she going to talk about? My mother stepped to the microphone—they were able to lower it that far. She then proceeded to lecture the Order of Evangelists on the importance of paying your tithing. She files her statement on January 1 each year, is annoyed that the Presiding Bishopric office is not open that day, and frets for hours if her calculations are off by twenty cents.

So what I am about to say is going to get me into a peck of trouble at Mom's house. But leadership requires courage that even means standing up to your 5' 1" mother. The way we are currently understanding the principle of tithing is no longer adequate to the needs of the church or the complex world in which we live. Don't misunderstand me. The principle of the tithe is a sound biblical concept absolutely essential to the well-being of the church. (Mom, now being resuscitated somewhere in the balcony, has just emitted a deep sigh of relief.)

But, friends, we urgently need a creative, scripturally sound, globally applicable theology of stewardship that lifts us beyond forms and formulas and gets us to the fundamental connection between the sharing of the tithe and the path of the disciple. A major assessment is already under way and some preliminary conclusions have been reached. We will engage the church in a dialogue about that over the coming months, and we invite all of you to join with us in that process.

2. What things have people shared with you and how has their giving helped you?

3. Discuss the meaning and implications of "merging the function of the steward with the heart of the disciple."

4. What principles would you include in a "creative, scripturally sound, globally applicable theology of stewardship"?

5. Think of a relationship in which you give generously, willingly, and consistently. What motivates you to give that way?

Scripture Study

> Blessed be the God and Father of our Lord Jesus Christ, the Father of mercies and the God of all consolation, who consoles us in all our affliction, so that we may be able to console those who are in any affliction with the consolation which we ourselves are consoled by God.
>
> —II Corinthians 1:3–4

6. We are called to give willingly out of the blessings of our lives. When one has received comfort in a time of great distress, it becomes a gift to share with another whose life feels shattered because of tragedy or turmoil. What are some of the gifts for which you are grateful and which you must share with others?

> Therefore I tell you, do not worry about your life, what you will eat or what you will drink, or about your body, what you will wear. Is not life more than food, and the body more than clothing? Look at the birds of the air; they neither sow nor reap nor gather into barns, and yet your heavenly Father feeds them. Are you not of more value than they? And can any of you by worrying add a single hour to your span of life? And why do you worry about clothing? Consider the lilies of the field, how they grow; they neither toil nor spin, yet I tell you, even Solomon in all his glory was not clothed like one of these. But if God so clothes the grass of the field, which is alive today and tomorrow is thrown into the oven, will he not much more clothe you—you of little faith? Therefore do not worry, saying, "What will we eat?" or "What will we drink?" or "What will we wear?" For it is the Gentiles who strive for all these things; and indeed your heavenly Father knows that you need all these things. But strive first for the kingdom of God and his righteousness, and all these things will be given to you as well.
>
> —Matthew 6:25–33

7. How do you balance having faith that "God will provide" with accepting personal responsibility to provide for your own needs and the needs of your family? How do we determine what is a reasonable standard of living for our own family as we struggle with questions regarding how much we should share from our personal resources?

> [S]eek ways of effecting a greater understanding of the meaning of the stewardship of temporalities as a response to my grace and love.
>
> —Doctrine and Covenants 154:5a

8. If we acknowledge the rich blessings we are given by God, it is only natural to be moved by the recognition of that grace to share our abundance with those we encounter. What interferes with our willingness to share abundant blessings with those around us and in other parts of our world?

> These are portentous times. The lives of many are being sacrificed unnecessarily to the gods of war, greed, and avarice. The land is being desecrated by the thoughtless waste of vital resources. You must obey my commandments and be in the forefront of those who would mediate this needless destruction while there is yet day.
>
> —Doctrine and Covenants 150:7

9. We share in the sense of being just one small part of God's interdependent creation. As we consider the discipline of sharing, what implications does this have as we decide how and what we will "take" out of God's creation? How can the language of sharing be useful in developing a more holistic view of our place in the world?

Exploring Sharing

One evening in the height of the Pokemon craze, my young son, Ross, and I [Anita Mortimer] were at a fast-food restaurant. A free Pokemon figure was being given away with every kid's meal, so there we were, both eating our kids' meals so that he could have two of the prized figurines. A few tables away from us there sat a young father and his son. They were sharing a sandwich and two glasses of water. It seemed fairly obvious to me that even this meager feast was purchased at some sacrifice to their budget. I surmised, rightly or wrongly, that on this rainy evening, this was a place the father had chosen because it offered them a warm place to come and play and spend some time together, but only if they purchased at least one sandwich as their supper.

As we ate our food and they theirs, Ross began to realize that this young boy had no kid's meal and, therefore, no Pokemon toy. He commented on that fact to me, and I agreed that was the case. He got up from his seat, went to the boy, and asked, "Don't you like Pokemon?" before I could impose my more civilized reluctance upon him. The boy answered that he did, and his head hung slightly as he responded. The man put his arm across his son's shoulder in a show of comfort, and I had the feeling there had been some discussion of the toys between them earlier.

Ross returned to our table and took the two toys we had gotten with our meals in his hands. He stroked and gazed at each for a moment. One he had already had at home. The other was one he had been hoping to get but, until today, without success. I was sure he was considering giving the duplicate toy to the young boy and hoped he would reach that conclusion himself. He looked at me with very serious eyes. I said nothing. It was his choice, and he knew that. Suddenly he took the toy he had been hoping to get in his hand and moved to the other table. Presenting it to the young boy, he said, "This one has great powers. Would you like to have it?" The little boy's face became bright with joy. He looked at his father, who looked at me. I simply nodded with a smile, and the man said OK to his son.

When Ross returned to our table, I told him I was so very proud of his choice, but I had to ask, "What made you offer the one you'd been hoping to get?"

Ross replied, "I have lots of Pokemon things. This may be the only one that little boy ever gets. If you only have one Pokemon, it should be one with great powers."

Children may not have a good reputation for sharing, but often they are far better at it than those of us who claim to be their examples. Have you ever watched a group of children dividing up some yummy morsel to share with one another? They are often meticulous about making sure the portions are precisely measured. At other times, they recognize the logic of a particular person getting slightly more than what seems to adults as their appropriate share. I was once responsible for dishing up ice cream at a certain function. A small hand tugged at my jacket, and when I bent to listen to the request, I was asked to give a little extra to a certain child. "His mommy is really sick," the little messenger whispered. "He could use some cheering up."

I was raised with what I now realize is the almost universal system for dividing things among siblings. One divides; the other chooses. If it is a candy bar, one child cuts it in half (or thirds or whatever the required number of pieces); the other chooses first. It works amazingly well to assure fair distribution of limited resources. It seems so universally applied, I have about concluded it is a system placed into the universal subconscious. So perhaps it is the way things are intended to be distributed—whoever divides the resource must let all others choose first.

But we have somehow gotten it twisted. It seems more and more clear that we have set our world up in ways that allow those who do the dividing to also choose first. It often doesn't work very well. Perhaps when we look at the various resources necessary to life, we should learn to evaluate each of our "takings" on the basis of whether we would be satisfied to take the smallest piece left after everyone else had already chosen. If not, perhaps there is a problem with the distribution.

10. How could you apply the universal system of dividing (one divides, the other chooses) to the following resources?
food resources
health care
education
power to determine own future
the gospel
Using each of those examples, then decide the following.
Who is doing the dividing?
On what basis is the division made?
Would you be satisfied with the smallest portion?

Feeding the 5,000[28]

The only miracle story told in all four Gospels, with the exception of the resurrection itself, is the feeding of the 5,000. I [Anita Mortimer] once listened as someone explained to me that it wasn't a miracle at all. What really happened, this person insisted, was that most of the people there had little bits of food tucked away in their belongings, but they were choosing not to bring them out for fear of having to share with their neighbors. When they witnessed the unselfishness of the boy who presented the loaves and fishes (this person's theory only works with the version found in John 6), they were so moved that they all brought out and shared their food, and there was more than enough to go around.

If the unselfishness of one small boy was enough to inspire everyone in the crowd to spontaneously redistribute the wealth so that all had plenty, that is miracle enough for me. We live in a world that has more than enough for all who inhabit it, but we have not yet incorporated an understanding of that abundance into our lives in ways that inspire us to insist on equitable distribution.

11. Discuss situations where there would be more than enough for everyone if people would share what they have.

12. Read other accounts of feeding the multitude (for references, see endnote 28) and discuss what you think are important elements of the story.

Share Willingly from Our Blessings—Dave Nii[29]

One of the great life lessons I learned was triggered by my college freshman chemistry professor. Our class was expected to turn in homework assignments each class period, and, as often is the case with overconfident eighteen year olds, we vigorously protested this injustice because we were much too sophisticated to go along with this activity that reeked of high school. When confronted with this objection, our professor simply explained in his "that's just the way it is" tone, **"I want your hands to practice writing the correct answers."**

Out of that flippant remark, which he probably used every year on entering freshman, a truism struck, and stuck, with me.

No matter how sophisticated, intelligent, accomplished, or enlightened I think I am, I will simply be continuing in ignorance and arrogance unless my "hands continue to practice writing the correct answers" (i.e., unless my life, in thought and deed, continues to reflect my beliefs and understandings).

For me, this truism is what the "path of the disciple" describes. Our journey as transformed followers of the Christ must be one that imbeds our understanding of correct answers into our entire lives and beings and is continually reflected in our thoughts, words, and actions. To "share willingly from the blessings of our lives" is one of those understandings and values that I hope our faith community honestly embraces and grows in its practice. For me it is a restatement of the commandment, "You shall love your neighbor as yourself." To share our life's abundance so others may also be blessed is inseparable from our understanding of the gospel of Christ.

In my moments of doubt and frustration with the minutia of church administration, program planning, and a seemingly endless array of meetings, I am renewed when I remember my friends who have modeled the path of sharing in their lives. These exemplars share, not primarily because of their perceived wonderful end results, but because of the joy in the journey of sharing itself. Their sharing is not just something they do; it is at the heart of their discipleship, at the heart of their being. These are the people who provide the energy and hope that sustain congregations through difficult and frustrating times because they have grown to understand and live out lives of response that love others as they love themselves. These are the people who continue to practice writing the correct answers in their lives. The path of the disciple is to share willingly from the blessings of our lives. I celebrate our faith community's renewed focus on sharing as a way of life and look forward to finding ways to earnestly and actively convert this noble concept into our individual and corporate discipleship and being.

13. What are the barriers that might keep us from sharing? What do we need to do to remove these barriers?

14. Complete the following sentence on a 3"x5" card. Keep it with you and add specific plans for how you will share with others.

My greatest gifts for sharing are...

Partners with Creation

We have to consider how we share the earth (and beyond) and its resources with one another and with all God's creation. What implications does discipleship have for our stewardship of nature? Sharing isn't just about being fair or equitable in our decisions of what is mine and what belongs to another. Sharing is a recognition that we share in the sense of being together with one another and with creation in this place. Children sometimes have a much better grasp than we do of the truth that sharing is about all of life. Seeing a bit of trash being tossed from the window of a passing car window, my [Anita Mortimer] six year old commented, "It must just make God cry to see us treat the Earth that way." We often don't share creation responsibly.

> We give-away our thanks to the earth
>   which gives us our home.
> We give-away our thanks to the rivers and lakes
>   which give-away their water.
> We give-away our thanks to the trees
>   which give-away fruit and nuts.
> We give-away our thanks to the wind
>   which brings rain to water the plants.
> We give-away our thanks to the sun
>   who gives-away warmth and light.
> All beings on earth: the trees, the animals, the wind
>   and the rivers give-away to one another
>   so all is in balance.
> We give-away our promise to begin to learn
>   how to stay in balance with all the earth.[30]

15. Create a list of ways you can be a better steward of the Earth.

16. How many things on your list would help to create more resources for those who are without?

39

Living in Response to God's Grace—Gregg McDonald[31]

Many are familiar with *Les Misérables*, a novel by Victor Hugo (1888). It tells the story of a good man who stole in desperation and then spent years in prison. After his release, it appeared his life would simply be a new sort of prison, but an act of grace offered him new hope. The story of the impact of that act of grace is a wonderful one, but there is a deeper story to share about the person who bestowed grace on the good man in the novel. He was an old Roman Catholic bishop, Charles-Francois-Bienvenu Myriel. In the novel, the story relates that shortly after being installed as Bishop of Digne, a small French village, the bishop moved into the finely appointed palace designated as his home. He later went to visit a hospital nearby. It was a cramped, run-down facility housing far more patients than it had beds or space. Observing the plight of the patients and hospital workers, the bishop declared that there had been a mistake—somehow he had been given the space intended for the hospital, and they had been placed in the space intended for him. He made arrangements to move into the hospital quarters and for the hospital to be moved into his palace.

In a major Midwestern city, a young man in his twenties was chosen by Habitat for Humanity as the recipient of one of their houses. The young man worked side by side with the Habitat volunteers. On the day the house was dedicated, the young man announced that he had asked his eighty-year-old grandmother to live with him there. He spoke of how blessed he was to have such a lovely home and said he wanted to share it with someone who had been important to him all his life. He was thrilled that he could now share something with her.

17. In your culture, what things tell you that someone is important? How are these the same or different from the stories we have just read? Who is important in the kingdom of God that we read about in the Gospels?

18. What are some of the things we must be aware of or precautions we should take when sharing with others? What is different about the approach organizations such as Outreach International or Habitat for Humanity take in helping people and the approach taken by some welfare programs?

Joy in Sharing

Jeff Brumbeau and Gail de Marcken collaborated on a beautiful children's story about the joy of sharing. It is titled *The Quiltmaker's Gift.*[32]

Once there was a quiltmaker who lived high in the misty mountains. She made the prettiest quilts ever seen. The world's people climbed to her home in the mountains hoping to buy one of her magnificent quilts. But she told them her quilts were her gifts to the poor; they were not for the rich. On the darkest, coldest nights, the woman would go into the villages and lay her quilts gently on those sleeping out in the cold, then tiptoe away.

One day the powerful and greedy king decided that the one thing he did not possess and that would make him happy was one of the woman's quilts. He went with his soldiers to the woman's home in the misty mountains, but when he demanded one of her quilts, she said they were only for the poor. The quiltmaker told the king that if he gave away all his things, she would present him with a quilt.

Never! None of the king's threats or punishments could make her give him a quilt. Finally, in desperation, he searched for one thing he might be able to give away. He was only able to part with one tiny object, but the smile on the face of the lad who received it inspired the king to find more things to give away, and finally, the joy on the faces of the people to whom he gave his things moved him to travel the world giving away all the fine things he had collected.

When he returned to the quiltmaker's home, she said that since he was now poor himself, she would give him a quilt. "But I am not poor," he said. "I may look poor, but in truth my heart is full to bursting, filled with memories of all the happiness I've given and received. I'm the richest man I know." But the quiltmaker had made this special quilt just for the king, and he accepted her gift to him. Each night he returned to the quiltmaker's home so that he could take a quilt to the village and have the joy of giving it away.

19. Have there been times in your life when you were truly able to experience joy in giving?

41

20. The king had great wealth, but he was unhappy. What is the value of things in our lives? What purpose do they serve for us? In what ways do they interfere with our happiness?

The Community of Christ has its own "quiltmaker" story. Margie is a church member in Boulder, Colorado. She was intrigued by the stories she'd heard of quilting bees—coming together for devotions and fellowship and good labor. She found herself thinking it would be a good experience for people to come together in the spirit of worship and fellowship, make something really beautiful, and then give it away. It is hard to give away something you have worked so hard on and something you appreciate as a thing of beauty. She thought the whole experience would be of value to those involved. She began to piece together tops for crib quilts—lots of them. A church appointee mentioned children in an orphanage for whom those quilts would be a real blessing.

Eventually some students at Graceland University became involved. Margie pieced the tops with help from family and friends. The quilts then went to Graceland where students came together to talk and worship and tie quilts. Then the quilts traveled back to Colorado for the finishing touches and to be packaged for shipment to the orphanage. Each person who worked on a quilt shared a bit of themselves with a lonely child who desperately needed to be wrapped in God's love.

Another church member makes quilts that are truly stunning works of art and donates each one to a charitable cause. In some cases, the quilts have been sold at charity auctions to raise money that later provides needed services.

21. We've all heard the expression "labor of love." What can we gain by working hard to create something we know we are going to give away?

22. What are some of the ways you share? Which of these give you the most satisfaction?

Sharing the Gospel: The Green Tomato Missionary—
Bob Kyser

The large paved parking lot adjoining the Shawnee Drive Congregation in Shawnee Mission, Kansas, is a great place to ride bikes. One day Sean, a boy from the neighborhood, grew tired of riding (including some trips through the flower garden) and decided to pass the time throwing green tomatoes against the side of the church building. The tomatoes had been planted by one of the Sunday school classes in order to watch them grow.

Paul was inside cleaning the church when he heard the "thump, thump, thump" against the wall. Going outside to investigate, he found Sean. They visited, and Paul invited Sean to come to church. Several days later Sean met the pastor, Brenda. Again he was invited to church. Brenda told him that the congregation does lots of eating, especially on Wednesday nights, and they would love for him to come. The congregation had planned a vacation church school for Wednesday nights in September. They made a point of inviting Sean to attend. The first night he brought his girlfriend and two other girls. The girls, in turn, invited others, and each night the attendance grew—eleven new children attended.

The young adults accepted the responsibility of continuing this missionary opportunity with a meal, Bible stories, games, and crafts each Wednesday night. This group of children prepared a Christmas pageant for the entire congregation as well as for their parents and families.

Brenda summarized, "We believe that God sent Sean and his friends to Shawnee Drive. They did what we were unable to do—they brought us children with whom to share the gospel. We praise God for this opportunity and hope and pray that we will be able to continue this ministry to our neighborhood."

23. This could easily have been a "missed opportunity" for sharing the gospel. There were a number of instances when a different response could have ended the sharing. What are some of those moments? What are situations in your own life where a slight change in your response might provide an opportunity to share the gospel?

Conclusion

To walk the path of the disciple is to share willingly from the blessings of our lives. Of our heritage, Grant McMurray reminded us, "we had all things in common and then evolved the principles of tithing and stewardship."[33] Can we envision a future in which our heartfelt response to God's grace enables all to enjoy the abundant resources of Earth in ways that meet needs and enrich lives?

Closing

Sing together "Creator of Sunrises," *Hymns of the Saints* (*HS* 186), and close with prayer focused on the call to share willingly.

Chapter 4

Learn
and Teach

Key Scripture

Be respectful of tradition. Do not fail to listen attentively to the telling of the sacred story, for the story of scripture and of faith empowers and illuminates. But neither be captive to time-bound formulas and procedures. Remember that instruction given in former years is applicable in principle and must be measured against the needs of a growing church, in accordance with the prayerful direction of the spiritual authorities and the consent of the people.

—Doctrine and Covenants 161:5

1. How does your congregation tell the sacred story? Be specific. Are there additional methods to tell the sacred story that could be learned and used effectively?

2. When have you seen yourself or a group bound by formulas and procedures that were out-dated? Or when have you seen a present situation guided by principles given in another time?

A Call to Discipleship—Grant McMurray[34]

Fourth, the path of the disciple requires us to be learners and teachers. Many of us live in a world of soundbytes, media imagery, and information that comes in very short bursts. We have lost a sense of history. We settle for the superficial and the trite and call that knowledge. We let television networks and talk show hosts define our beliefs, want pamphlets instead of books, and declare resources to be without merit if they are

45

not filled with pictures. I understand the importance of presentation, of design and visuals. But the disciple has to be concerned about content and meaning. We must get past the surface and invest ourselves deeply in the particulars of our faith so that we are not just willing disciples but competent ones as well.

To do so requires a careful reassessment of the Sunday school, which each year is becoming a weaker and weaker component of church life. A new vitality and energy must go into preparing ourselves for discipleship. If that requires a revamping of the Sunday school format, so be it. If that requires having some people step forward and say "I'll do it!" then let's get off our haunches and get it done.

But more is required… I announce our intention to launch a five-year program, jointly engaged in by the World Church and local congregations, that has at its heart the imperative of making us a more scripturally literate people. To do so is to buck the trend of a culture where a dominant number of people seem to think Joan of Arc is married to Noah. Jay Leno's man-on-the-street interviews about biblical understandings depict the paucity of knowledge about even the basic Bible stories, things that once provided images and symbols common to all.

It is critically important that we continue to develop the Transformation 2000 objective of developing a theology of peace and justice "based on the scriptures, faith, and traditions of the Restoration movement." If we fail to do that work we will have simply created a call to social do-goodism that is without roots and devoid of the deeper call to embody the ministries of the Christ. To call the church to scriptural literacy is not at all to embrace a moribund fundamentalism that creates a life theology out of a handful of biblical quotations. To follow the road to a stifling literalism imprisons the scriptures in a cage and refuses to let them breathe and evolve as our lives listen to them in new ways.

Instead, we must develop a theology of scripture that appreciates the richness and depth of the sacred Word and points to the eternal truths that lurk behind its parables and stories and mythical abstractions. It is especially important for a church that claims more than one book of scripture and professes belief in continuing revelation to formulate a sound theology of the Word that allows room for God to speak through both ancient and contemporary forms.

We begin by committing ourselves to develop programs of scriptural literacy that train our children, build a foundation for our youth, deepen and enrich the understandings of adults, and assure all of us that what we do is founded on God's Word.

But even that is not enough to make us the trained disciples we are called to become. In a couple of days we will introduce a piece of legislation that asks the World Conference to approve the initial steps toward establishment of a seminary to train those who wish to engage in full-time ministry or to enhance their self-sustaining ministry in this faith community.

I grew up in congregations led by wonderful men who felt that preparation for worship was simply to let the Spirit work its wonders. My experience was that sometimes the Spirit made a miraculous appearance and sometimes it decided that today it would work with those who had prepared a bit more. Occasionally the Spirit has bailed me out when I wasn't ready, but it usually finds a pretty direct way of reminding me that being an effective witness may sometimes be about miracles but more often it is about preparation.

We have completed two years of study and discussion and believe we are ready to launch an initiative to establish a seminary for the benefit of the church. We intend to use partnerships with Graceland [University] and with other institutions of higher education to harness the amazing technologies of distance learning and Internet education, and utilize the broad skill base of talents we have among church members around the globe.

3. List the ways (resources and situations) in which you learn. When have you had an important learning experience that came from an unexpected source?

4. What should be the goal of learning and teaching in the context of discipleship? in the church?

5. List all of the ways we experience Christian education. What are the potential benefits of Christian education? What keeps

our Christian education from being merely a "sharing of our ignorance"?

6. Assist the World Church by envisioning new plans for Christian education. In small groups, create plans for Christian education that might revitalize the church school or go beyond it. What needs to change in order to create an atmosphere of learning within your congregation? Each group will then share their plans with the whole group. You may come up with some ideas you will want to try in your congregation and then share those successes with the World Church Peace and Justice Team, which provides adult study materials.

7. What does it mean to be scripturally literate? Why is scripture study important?

8. What stumbling blocks do people encounter in the study of scripture? How can these be overcome?

9. What will we need to study and understand in order to develop a theology of peace and justice? What steps can you take to move the process along for yourself and your congregation?

Scripture Study

After three days they found him in the temple, sitting among the teachers, listening to them and asking them questions.

—Luke 2:46

10. We usually think of the story of Jesus in the temple from the standpoint of Jesus as teacher. But this verse catches up another aspect of his needing to be in God's house—he was talking with the wise men of the time and *"listening to them and asking them questions."* Can you think of a particular time when you gained new insight as you listened to someone else? When have you asked questions in an effort to better understand someone's perspective or viewpoint? Have you ever had the experience of having your mind totally changed about an issue because you were willing to be open to someone else's ideas or perspective?

Therefore, verily I say unto you, my friends, Call your solemn assembly, as I have commanded you; and as all have not faith, seek ye diligently and

48

teach one another words of wisdom; yea, seek ye out of the best books words of wisdom; seek learning even by study, and also by faith.
—Doctrine and Covenants 85:36a

And verily I say unto you, that it is my will that you should hasten to . . . obtain a knowledge of history, and of countries, and of kingdoms, of laws of God and man, and all this for the salvation of Zion.
—Doctrine and Covenants 90:12

[The Temple] shall be the means for providing leadership education for priesthood and member.
—Doctrine and Covenants 156:5d

Dear Saints, have courage for the task which is yours in bringing to pass the cause of Zion. Prepare yourselves through much study and earnest prayer.
—Doctrine and Covenants 156:11a

Instruction which has been given in former years is applicable in principle to the needs of today and should be so regarded by those who are seeking ways to accomplish the will of their heavenly Father. But the demands of a growing church require that these principles shall be evaluated and subjected to further interpretation. This requisite has always been present. In meeting it under the guidance of my spirit, my servants have learned the intent of these principles more truly.
—Doctrine and Covenants 147:7

11. The call to the discipline of learning is not new in the Restoration. In what ways has the church as an institution emphasized the importance of study and learning?

12. When have you felt the conflict between the obvious call to the discipline of learning that has been present throughout our movement's history and the importance we have placed on the movement of the Spirit?

Exploring Learning and Teaching

Once or twice a week, I [Anita Mortimer] drive a few minutes to a nearby elementary school to have lunch with a group of young students. It is always a bit of an adventure. I can't help being struck by the sheer love of learning I encounter in that cafeteria. There is an exhilaration that is hard to describe. The world is still a relatively new place to these young adventurers, and they have not yet lost the thrill of discovering and sharing its secrets. They are not just excited to learn a few new facts; rather, they are excited because they sense that their lives are being transformed by their learning. They realize that new worlds are open and available to them as they learn to apply the principles they are mastering to new situations they encounter. Hopefully, we will allow ourselves to be caught up in that love of learning and then teach others what we've learned.

Most of us (I really think all of us, but I have a very hard time with "all" or "none" statements!) had that excitement of learning at one time in our lives, and for reasons we do not even understand, many of us let it slip away. Occasionally I encounter an adult who enthusiastically approaches new information, new areas of interest, or new understandings of familiar concepts.

A friend shared a story about a woman in her nineties who decided to go back to college. She was a valuable and much loved member of every class she took. Her openness to learning new things and sharing what she had learned along her life's journey was an inspiration to the young adults who shared her classrooms. The vacant seat that confronted her classmates after her death was a reminder to all of them that learning must never stop. I'd like to think my death, whenever it comes, will leave an empty seat in some classroom.

13. What keeps the love of learning alive in us? What destroys it?

14. What have been some things you learned in your life that needed to be rethought or adjusted at a later time? How did you feel about having to change in this way?

15. What are some tools we should use or questions we should ask when confronted with new ideas that may not match the beliefs we hold?

16. Name some of the great learners and teachers you have known. Describe them and the impact they have had on others.

17. What does it mean to learn and teach in the context of discipleship? What is the difference between learning a new fact and being transformed by new ideas?

Learning: An Expanded Reflection—Frank Kelley[35]

All men by nature desire to know.—Aristotle[36]

I do not feel obliged to believe that that same God who has endowed us with sense, reason, and intellect has intended us to forgo their use.—Galileo[37]

I am learning all the time. The tombstone will be my diploma.—Eartha Kitt[38]

Learning is a relatively permanent change in behavior or in behavioral potentiality that results from experience and cannot be attributed to temporary body states such as those induced by illness, fatigue, or drugs.—B. R. Hergenhahn[39]

It is often a desire of denominations to seek solid positions on religious matters so as to be grounded and sure in principle and program. The role of learners and learning has been consistent in its presence in our church's history and tradition. We have, however, had to constantly shore up defenses against the tides of a secular culture on one hand and a wave of persistent anti-intellectualism on the other. Strangers' voices decried the search for the sacred, while in our own camp, for too long, we heard the claim that only the presence of the Spirit was required as compass and guide in the trek to the New Jerusalem.

We have attempted to address the business of educating our people in those areas deemed truly necessary for the life of a disciple. Challenged to develop a theology of scripture, we are exploring the possibilities of ratcheting up the process in the areas of the church school, seminary training, and individual study.

The current culture—a tyranny of trivia—constantly distracts even the best intentioned from the possibilities of the kind of intellectual development promoted by Paul when he urged Timothy to *"present yourself to God as one approved"* (II Timothy 2:15) and by the young prophet when he counseled the Saints to *"study and learn,"* for the *"glory of God is intelligence"* (Doctrine and Covenants 87:5b, 90:6a).

I would suggest a wider perspective and a press for "a theology of learning." Such a search would most certainly include

51

holy writ but would move far in the direction of the growth and maturity required for such a time as this. Just three reasons— among many—for broadening the effort will suffice to articulate the challenge. First, learning is great sport and a joy in the full sense declared by Lehi (II Nephi 1:115). The joy of learning compounds over time in ways that are truly enriching. Second, the process of seeking learning over a wide range of interests brings a maturing reward in and through the fruits of reflection and contemplation. Third, the process of learning on the scope described in the Doctrine and Covenants cited above equips us in special ways to be and serve and grow. We live in a time and in a world that desperately seeks and requires persons who are able to match these moments. Václav Havel, president of the Czech Republic, wrote in *The Futurist*:

> **And thus today we find ourselves in a paradoxical situation. We enjoy all the achievements of modern civilization that have made our physical existence on this earth easier in so many important ways. Yet we do not know exactly what to do with ourselves, where to turn. The world of our experiences seems chaotic, disconnected, confusing. There appear to be no integrating forces, no unified meaning, no true inner understanding of phenomena in our experience of the world. Experts can explain anything in the objective world to us, yet we understand our own lives less and less. In short, we live in the postmodern world, where everything is possible and almost nothing is certain.[40]**

Facing such a time and living in such a world, it would be normal to seek simple, and simplistic, solutions. To set "learning" up as a cure-all or, worse, as the cure-all for our concerns and challenges would be a serious mistake. But not to embrace the possibilities of learning as a life-long effort would be an error for which we would pay too dearly.

A theology of learning must embrace the truths of scripture. But to realize the vast potential for delight and joy, the fruits of reflection and maturing contemplation, and the possibilities of lasting accomplishment, a skilled and learned people will demand and require more. With as wide and deep an understanding as possible, ours is an attainable dream and one of the great and marvelous things awaiting us beyond the horizon.

Light comes from learning—just as creation comes everywhere—through integrations, syntheses, not through exclusions.—Eduard Lindeman[41]

18. Where do we find guidance on the path to becoming disciples?

19. What are the circumstances in which you learn best? Is it the same as others in the class? What does this tell us about Christian education?

20. When have you experienced learning as a "great sport" bringing joy that "compounds over time"?

21. Read Doctrine and Covenants 85:21 and discuss the scope of topics suggested in light of our desire to develop a theology of peace and justice and in light of our mission to "proclaim Jesus Christ and promote communities of joy, hope, love, and peace."

22. Identify some specific ways you are better equipped to grow in the expression of your discipleship.

23. What would your theology of learning include?

Seek Learning by Study and Faith—Joey Williams

PARIS, FRANCE—Most people dream about living in a foreign country, but on a hot September morning, my dream became my reality. I stepped down from the bus gazing at the glass-pyramid entrance of the Louvre Museum, humbled by the grandeur of this awe-inspiring city. That wasn't the only thing that humbled me though—I stepped right into a pile of doggy doo! Now, I'm not sure if this was a way of preparing me for the next few months or not, but it was definitely an accurate foretelling of some of the experiences that followed.

Nothing went right in Paris. I didn't have the right papers, I was set up in the wrong school program, and my host family treated me poorly. I wanted to go home. Then I received a letter from a youth who had been in my cabin at senior high camp. He wrote how "cool" it was that I was in France, learning French. I thought, "if he only knew." He ended the letter with a scripture I had used when he was in junior high:

I thank my God every time I remember you, constantly praying with joy in every one of my prayers for all of you, because of your sharing in the gospel from the first day until now. I am confident of this, that the one who began a good work among you will bring it to completion by the day of Jesus Christ.

—Philippians 1:3–6

Was Christ there for me in France? I was miserable. What purpose did I have in France? I began to replace my solitude with study and faith. I studied God's word and worked hard to learn French. I had faith that God's purpose would be revealed to me.

A few months later, I left Paris. One beautiful spring evening, I found myself sitting around a table in Toulon, a small French town on the Mediterranean. The appointee for the Europe Region had come to discuss the work of the church in France with a small group of church people. One catch—he didn't speak any French, and they didn't speak any English. As I struggled through translation and the emotions of a group debating issues of church formation, I was overcome by a sense of the Spirit. Two things had brought me to this point in my life: Study had prepared me for the work, and faith had led me to the opportunity to fulfill that work.

Today, three years later, I am in my final semester toward my master's degree in French. I study in faith, knowing that God has a work for me and will continue to direct me until that work is complete. Seek learning by study and faith, and you will be amazed at how God will use you for the building of God's kingdom here on Earth.

24. Describe instances in which you have experienced the reward of having prepared well for a particular endeavor. When have there been times in your life when only hindsight permitted you to see the value of some learning you had undertaken? Or describe a time when you were able to fill a vital role because of some training you had or when you were able to provide a special ministry because of study you had undertaken without fully understanding how it would be useful in your life.

Responsible Christianity

I [Anita Mortimer] remember sitting in a scripture study class many years ago. There was a heated debate about the meaning of a certain passage. How it was interpreted had significant implications for how several members of this particular group would respond to a situation confronting them. A young woman who sat without comment through most of the group's weekly sessions shyly made a suggestion. Perhaps, she offered, there was a commentary or other resource that would assist us in understanding what the passage meant. I am sad to report that her suggestion was soundly rejected. Everything the group needed to understand about the passage, the group's leader insisted, was right there in the book itself. Our task was to be open to the truth it contained, not to search "extraneous" material looking for excuses or justifications for behavior we found difficult to eliminate from our lives.

After a few more sessions of debate, the individuals faced with this difficult situation made a decision regarding how they would respond that was based upon the "majority opinion" about the meaning of this passage. The course of action they chose totally devastated a family member and irreparably divided their family. It seemed most unchristian.

As I reflect on that experience now, I sadly realize that the group, which was striving sincerely to honor Restoration scriptures, missed a central theme—the instruction to study and seek all available light. As a group, we also failed to read the particular passage that concerned us in light of the life of Jesus who so fully honored the worth of all.

In the book *Remedial Christianity,* Paul Laughlin wrote of the central role of the Bible in Christian faith. As appropriate as that centrality is, he wrote, the irony is that "no aspect of Christianity is more misunderstood and misused by Christians themselves than the Bible."[42] Laughlin wrote of Bible study among Christians usually amounting to no more than "a mere sharing of impressions by well-intentioned, but woefully uninformed people."[43] His comments brought the image of that "study group" from my youth lurching painfully into my mind.

Careful study of scripture can be transforming. As we grapple with what the scriptures mean to us and how we should apply them in our lives, it may be important for us not to view the Bible as *only* "a message for us and our day—a kind of timeless telegram from God—with little concern for the context in which it was written or the intent of its author."[44] We have available to us the benefit of extensive biblical scholarship—some of it excellent, some of it not. To remain "woefully uninformed" about something so central to our faith as the Bible is inexcusable. The study of the Doctrine and Covenants is enhanced by a good understanding of history and the issues that were being addressed at the time each section was given. New insights and excitement come when the Bible is read with an understanding of the issues and context of those people. Without the availability of this kind of background, our approach to the Book of Mormon may be somewhat different. But there are many approaches to scripture study and ways of appreciating and using the truth and inspiration revealed there.

As Apostle Bunda Chibwe once so appropriately commented, when we are dealing with scripture, we must be willing to understand what is the letter and what is the envelope. What is the divine principle that deserves and requires our adherence, and what is the cultural fabric in which it is being delivered?

25. What resources would you need to make personal scripture study more fruitful?

26. How does Bible scholarship enrich our study of the Bible? What precautions would you follow regarding books written about the Bible?

The Importance of Scripture—Andrew Bolton

As an altar boy in the Catholic Church, scripture washed over me weekly as passages from the Bible were read at the Sunday mass in a small Catholic Church in rural Lancashire, England. When I went to Wye College, the School of Agriculture for the University of London, I was befriended by an older Methodist student who introduced me to fellowship and Bible reading in a more intentional way. I did not understand the Bible as well as many other students and was challenged to begin reading it more seriously. The stories of Jesus and the parables were reasonably familiar from my Catholic upbringing, but other passages were difficult for me to get hold of, but I persisted.

After my first year in college, I spent the summer in Oregon in the United States of America on a lily farm. It was a wonderful summer. I took the New Testament with me to read on this adventure. I was also introduced to the Book of Mormon. Crossing the United States from Sacramento, California, to New York City, New York, I read part of the Book of Mormon on the bus. I remember putting it to one side from time to time and thinking, "This is true! This is inspired!" Then I got bogged down in all the battles in Alma, and it was another two years before I read the entire Book of Mormon. By this time I had met the RLDS Church and was also introduced to a deeper Christian fellowship than I had experienced prior to this time. I then read the Doctrine and Covenants, this time by candlelight in the Canary Islands, Spain. Again I felt I was reading something that was inspired.

Since these beginnings, my love and appreciation of scripture have continued to grow. Reading the work of scholars has been a blessing, but I have found no substitute for studying scripture firsthand myself and, best of all, with others. I have found that I cannot be a faithful disciple of Jesus without diligent scripture study, the fellowship of fellow believers, and an openness to the Holy Spirit. In the first months after my RLDS baptism, scripture and other people's testimonies helped me discover who Jesus is really and wonderfully. Scripture and experiences in our international church have challenged my British cultural assumptions about racism, ethnocentricity, the poor, nationalism, the use of violence, and other abuses that dehumanize or diminish the equal worth of all persons in the sight of God. While all scripture is important, I have found that some scripture is more important than others. The New Testament, particularly the Gospels and the Sermon on the Mount, have become for me the most important scriptures and the key to reading aright other scriptures, whether from the Old Testament or the Book of Mormon or the Doctrine and Covenants. I am grateful to be a part of a Christian movement that is enriched by wonderful scriptures and is open to more light and truth from God. It is my conviction that without the stories of scripture, we cannot challenge the stories of our culture that betray the equal worth of all persons. We cannot be a faithful peace church without being soaked in the stories of Jesus and the early disciples, joining in the covenant of baptism with others, and opening ourselves to the promptings of the Holy Spirit.

I have been blessed with marvelous educational opportunities. Yet my evangelist's blessing continues to challenge me, "In all your learning, learn of Jesus."

27. What have been some of the difficulties you have encountered in scripture study? What have been some of the benefits you have enjoyed?

28. What is the role of faith in the whole process of learning? Why do you say that?

29. In your own discipleship or ministry, what are some current learning needs you have?

30. How might the church's dream of having our own seminary impact you? If you could take any course about any subject with the goal of improving your own ministry, what would you choose?

Conclusion

To walk the path of the disciple requires us to be learners and teachers. Early in our history, in a proclamation to all the world of the importance of learning and teaching, "We built a temple in Kirtland and called it a house of study, a house of prayer."[45] Are we diligent in our pursuit of insight and understanding?

Closing

Sing together "God Has Spoken through the Ages," *Hymns of the Saints* (*HS* 306), and close with prayer focused on the call to be learners and teachers.

Chapter 5

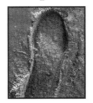

Engage in the Spiritual Quest

Key Scripture

Claim your unique and sacred place within the circle of those who call upon the name of Jesus Christ. Be faithful to the spirit of the Restoration, mindful that it is a spirit of adventure, openness, and searching. Walk proudly and with a quickened step. Be a joyful people. Laugh and play and sing, embodying the hope and freedom of the gospel.

Fulfill the purposes of the Temple by making its ministries manifest in your hearts....

The Spirit of the One you follow is the spirit of love and peace. That Spirit seeks to abide in the hearts of those who would embrace its call and live its message. The path will not always be easy, the choices will not always be clear, but the cause is sure and the Spirit will bear witness to the truth, and those who live the truth will know the hope and the joy of discipleship in the community of Christ. Amen.

—Doctrine and Covenants 161:1b; 2b; 3b; 3d; 7

1. How would you describe a spiritual person? a healing person?

A Call to Discipleship—Grant McMurray[46]

Fifth, the path of the disciple takes us to the mountaintop or into the forests or alongside the oceans in search of the God who resides within our own souls. The hunger for the spiritual is deep and abiding in what seems a profoundly secular world. It is the irony of our time that a generation often described as not religious is also described as *very* spiritual. The problem is that churches are seen as being about "beliefs" and somehow the spiritual quest has been uncoupled from that and connected with a smorgasbord of pursuits of the holy inspired by everything from Eastern mystics to massage therapies to spiritually centered exercise programs. I don't seek to ridicule or diminish those, many of which may have perfectly good value for adherents. What I do propose is that we get serious about the spiritual quest, recognize that there are many bruised and broken hearts in need of healing, and come to terms with the fact that a great many of those require new insights into the way the Spirit works among us.

I would say that the least developed of the three Transformation 2000 goals is healing of the spirit. It is the one thing that many of us would agree most needs to happen and perhaps the one thing that we seem least able to get our arms around. It's time to push the limits a bit and to consider the ways in which we limit the Spirit by assuming that the Spirit works only in certain ways. That Spirit has plunked me on the side of the head in some of the strangest situations and locations. I've argued with it a few times, declaring that it isn't supposed to show up here. And then magic happens and I recognize that I was the one boxing it up and holding back its healing and redeeming touch.

2. Do you know someone who is wounded in spirit? How have you worked to include that person in healing fellowship?

3. As a church we are committed to the following vision: "We will become a worldwide church dedicated to the pursuit of peace, reconciliation, and healing of the spirit." We have talked more about peace and reconciliation than healing of the spirit. In what kinds of situations do you see examples of the need for healing of the spirit? What resources are available to use in healing the spirits of people who are hurting? Which of the other disciplines under discussion also help with healing of the spirit?

4. In what ways can a person prepare to be an instrument of healing of the spirit?

5. Have you been surprised by how the Holy Spirit has worked with you or others? Describe the circumstances. What did you learn from that experience? What does this say about how we approach our spiritual quest?

Scripture Study

O LORD, you have searched me and known me.
You know when I sit down and when I rise up;
you discern my thoughts from far away.
You search out my path and my lying down,
and are acquainted with all my ways.
Even before a word is on my tongue,
O LORD, you know it completely.
You hem me in, behind and before,
and lay your hand upon me.
Such knowledge is too wonderful for me;
it is so high that I cannot attain it.

Where can I go from your spirit?
Or where can I flee from your presence?
If I ascend to heaven, you are there;
if I make my bed in Sheol, you are there.
If I take the wings of the morning
and settle in the farthest limits of the sea,
even there your hand shall lead me,
and your right hand shall hold me fast.
If I say, "Surely the darkness shall cover me,
and the light around me become night,"
even the darkness is not dark to you;
the night is as bright as the day, for darkness is as light to you.

For it was you who formed my inward parts;
you knit me together in my mother's womb.
I praise you, for I am fearfully and wonderfully made.
Wonderful are your works;
that I know very well.
How weighty to me are your thoughts, O God!
How vast is the sum of them!
I try to count them—they are more than the sand;
I come to the end—I am still with you.

—Psalm 139:1–14, 17–18

6. In what ways are this psalmist's comments about God true for you? What difference does it make in your life if you believe that God knows you completely and that you are always in God's presence?

So I say to you, Ask, and it will be given you; search, and you will find; knock, and the door will be opened for you.

—Luke 11:9

If any of you is lacking in wisdom, ask God, who gives to all generously and ungrudgingly, and it will be given you.

—James 1:5

7. What has been your experience of asking God for answers to important questions? In what ways has God provided answers to your questions?

Let my word be preached to the bruised and the brokenhearted as well as those who are enmeshed in sin, longing to repent and follow me.... My Spirit is reaching out to numerous souls even now and there are many who will respond.

—Doctrine and Covenants 153:9a, b

8. What is required of us by this scripture?
9. Why is it important that the bruised and brokenhearted hear the gospel?

Exploring Spiritual Quest

The first line of this section of President McMurray's sermon resounds with truth. We search our whole lives to find the God who is right there all the time.

I [Anita Mortimer] walked into the kitchen of a friend one evening. With her was a precious little three year old who had already encountered some pretty tough circumstances. My friend was kneeling in front of this small child. As I got closer, I was able to hear her say, "I just looked into your beautiful eyes, and do you know what I see in there? I see God in your eyes. God is in you, sure enough!" My friend was helping this little child find healing of the spirit.

It is appropriate to talk of the spiritual quest as a discipline. While there are occasions when a sense of communion with the Spirit seems to occur almost coincidentally, often our movement from a place of separation from God to one of connection comes through deliberate actions. A woman tells of the time in her marriage when she felt extreme strife and division. She was certain she knew the root of the conflict and was hurt and angry with the person she believed was responsible. She found herself so overwhelmed by her feelings that she could not even pray effectively about the situation or for that person. As a sort of "last resort," she wrote out a prayer for the person she believed was responsible for her pain, and she committed herself to reading that prayer aloud each morning. In that written prayer, she asked God to help the person to feel God's presence and sense God's great love.

It seemed almost silly—there was no sincerity in her voice as she read the words. More than once she decided there was no sense in reading a prayer she did not feel sincere about, but she had vowed to read it daily, and so she continued her practice. Over the course of many months, her heart was softened toward that person. She began to understand some of the hurt and brokenness that lay beneath that person's hurtful actions toward her.

In time she was able to pray sincerely for God's blessings for that individual. She invited God into her situation by an act of simple discipline. By submitting her brokenness to God's company and trusting God to understand the desires of her heart even more fully than she was able to, she emerged a more whole person. Eventually she was able to recognize the person she had once been unable to even pray for as a child of God. Her action of asking blessings instead of ill fortune eventually, through discipline, became the desire of her heart. She was blessed with a sense of wholeness and health that had once been drained from her by the conflict.

10. When have you had a changed attitude toward a person with whom you had difficulty? What factors or circumstances made the change in attitude possible?

Spirituality and the Church: Reflections for the Path Ahead—Dave Schaal[47]

Who Are the Hungry?

Typically, when we talk about spiritual formation ministries, we do so in regard to helping people **in the church** grow in their relationship with God. This is appropriate, of course, since matters of spirituality are central in the process of Christian maturation.

But what about people outside the fellowship of the church? In many places we continue to be aware of stories, reports, and merchandising efforts that suggest there is a spiritual hunger in the culture at large. It is noteworthy that this search for spiritual meaning is being voiced not only by "religious" folk, but by many people who are unattached to any faith community. For a church that is concerned about matters of both evangelism and spirituality, such reports about spiritual longings within the culture at large should grab our attention with considerable force. The question is, can we offer helps for the spiritual life that are intentionally designed for people outside our fellowship? Is it possible that some congregations or jurisdictional centers might become places known in their community as the place where people can go to learn the disciplines and relational practices associated with the healing of the spirit? Is it possible for the Temple itself to become known (dare we say marketed?) outside the church as a place where people may come to find training, resources, and support for the spiritual journey? What language would we need to learn in order to communicate this invitation to unchurched, spiritually searching persons? What training would we have to undertake to prepare ourselves for such a ministry?

This is not to suggest that we curtail efforts to help members of the church in their spiritual journey. It is simply to suggest that as we consider the matter of spirituality, we do so with our ears open to the needs outside church as well as within.

Engagement, Not Escape

For several years now, President McMurray has called us to become a prophetic people. If we look to the scriptures to ask what it means to be prophet-like, we discover that the prophets tended to be people who had one foot planted in an intimate relationship with God and the other foot planted in an intimate relationship with their culture. Their prophetic activity was an inspired effort to interpret the relationship between the two. Given our call to be a prophetic church, a significant question is: "Can our spirituality be one that deepens our relationship with God while also deepening our relationship with the world around us?"

The Saints in many places are surrounded with the voices of pop religious culture that suggest a spirituality that is, by its nature, **escapist**. These are the voices that encourage people to keep themselves pure by disengaging from a supposedly spiritually bankrupt world. These are the voices that would proclaim a stark separation between the physical and spiritual worlds, advocating that one should cling to the one and denounce the other.

In the Community of Christ, however, our attention to spirituality should honor our scriptural tradition that states that *"all things unto me are spiritual"* (Doctrine and Covenants 28:9a) and affirms that the world is not the enemy. Rather, the world is the arena where we are called to discern the Holy Spirit's presence. The world is the place where we are called to join God in meaningful work.

Tying our spirituality to the work of the peaceable community will be helpful to the Saints as we sort through the media hype that often portrays spirituality as something that disconnects us from the very world to which we are sent. Putting it positively, the spirituality of the church and the call to be prophetic should be closely aligned.

More Than Just Feeling

As a church, we have gone on record in stating our desire to embrace diversity. In matters of spirituality then, can we acknowledge the diversity of spiritual experience and orientation that is within our community?

Some time ago, I was at a fellowship service where the presider asked the question, "When was a time you felt the Holy Spirit?" In response, a number of people testified of occasions in which they felt the presence of God in their lives. While there was nothing wrong with this per se, it, nevertheless, was a service built upon the assumption that the Holy Spirit is something that is primarily *felt*. While it is certainly true that the Holy Spirit touches the human heart in a way that stirs feelings, a church that embraces diversity will also help people understand that "feeling" is only one modality through which the Spirit works to help us apprehend, communicate, and grow. As a church that affirms diversity, our spirituality can and should be one that gives place for the heart, embraces the intellect, affirms spontaneity and order, is informed by the physical world, and honors both knowledge and mystery.

Given our heritage and resources, the Community of Christ is uniquely postured to proclaim a more integrated spirituality that claims the whole person—body, mind, and spirit.

What about Our Theology?

While embracing diversity in the spiritual walk is important, it does not suggest a wholesale acceptance of everything that comes along under the banner of spirituality. It has been said that when a person is in the desert and thirsty, they will be drawn to whatever fountain springs up. Unfortunately, not all of the spiritual fountains springing up are particularly healthy. Some lead to exclusivism, wherein boxes are drawn around narrow definitions of how God's Spirit works and with whom God is willing to work. Others lead to spiritual addiction in which people run from experience to experience to get their spiritual "fix" that (like all addictions) prevents them from dealing with their own pain. At the other end of the spectrum, there are those who would understand spirituality as little more than a respect for the sanctity of life, but who would allow no possibility for actual interaction with an actual Spirit of an actual God.

Presently, spiritually searching people are wading through the waters of a hundred different currents of thought about the spiritual life. Some are wading in those waters alone; others have companions. Everyone who wades in, though, has some sorting out to do, and the sorting out can be confusing. Many times, people look to the church for guidance. In this regard, the church cannot engage in the simplistic notion of approving or disapproving every "school of spiritual thought" that comes along. On the other hand, is it possible for the church to engage in the theological task in a way that helps its members sort through the various messages that surround them? Obviously, this is no easy task, with no easy answers. However, the sound of the church's attempt to explore and articulate its theology should be ringing in people's ears at least as loudly as the theology of the evangelist on the local Christian radio station. The need is not to reach consensus on any given theological point. Instead, the need is to educate and model for the church the process of responsible, healthy theological exploration so that people may take those principles with them into the marketplace of ideas.

Initiate a New Emphasis or Create a New Culture?

As we enter a time in which we are speaking of the path of the disciple as a path that necessitates concern for spirituality, a very important question arises: "In reference to spirituality and the church, do we intend to initiate an emphasis, or do we intend to create a new culture within the life of the church?" The former is the easiest, of course. To initiate a new emphasis, we would produce several resources dealing with the spiritual life; write a *Herald* article or two; and promote the emphasis in our sermons, teaching, and other public ministries. These things are, of course, important and helpful.

Creating a new culture in the life of the church, though, is a greater challenge, since this has to do with "reframing" the behavior and practice that is expected of us in our day-to-day lives. Creating a new culture has to do with the priorities we set, what we model, how we interact, and what we practice in our personal and organizational lives.

It is not that we disbelieve the importance of spiritual practice, neither is it that we fail to be prayerful. It's just that it is so easy for deadlines, crowded schedules, and other institutional demands to take up a disproportionate amount of our time and energy. It is so easy for me to make the promise that I will give more attention to spiritual practice, just as soon as I get this one project behind me. Unfortunately, there are a hundred other projects in line and waiting for attention, each one adequately greased to slide into overloaded schedules before the promise of spiritual practice can be fulfilled.

The question is, can we create a climate in the life of the church wherein people find increasing encouragement and support for engagement in spiritual practice? For instance, suppose that you are a member of a congregational leadership team and month after month, you attend leadership meetings in which all of the time is spent in activity planning, budget management, and program development. The unspoken (but clear) message is that being a member of this leadership team means that you are expected to give attention to planning activities, managing budgets, and developing programs.

Where and how, though, do we set expectations that call for greater attention to the spiritual life? Obviously, each one of us is responsible for caring for our own spirituality, and we cannot depend upon others to do so. Is it possible, though, for us to create a different **culture of expectation** within the church— one in which we are expected to attach the same importance to prayer and thoughtful reflection as we give to meetings and other important matters?

Remember the Basics

We live in a time in which the idea of spiritual living is being applied to everything from quantum mechanics to the way we relate to our pets. This is appropriate and in many ways has been helpful (although I cannot speak for the pets). At the same time, in the presence of so many ways to talk about the spiritual life, there is something to be said about making sure that we do not forget the basic disciplines of personal spiritual practice. In our hurry-up world that strains for new technologies and new approaches to everything, it would be easy for us to forget to speak of such simple things as taking time out for personal prayer, meditation, and time with scripture. As we give increasing attention to matters of spirituality, may we remember to speak of such basic and necessary things.

As the Community of Christ, we are uniquely postured to proclaim a spirituality that is Christocentric, holistic, and out-reaching. Certainly there are many more thoughts and questions that could and should be discussed in regard to spirituality and church. The foregoing is offered simply as one small part in the ongoing discussion.

11. Do you see in society a spiritual longing? Give examples. What do people want and how can we help?

12. What do you see and hear through the media that portrays this spiritual yearning? Of the things you see, which may be helpful and which may be harmful for healing of the spirit? How has it changed through the years?

13. Who are the spiritual people you know? To what extent are they engaged with people and situations?

14. When have you experienced the Spirit of God in your life? Share these experiences in small groups and consider the diversity of experiences.

15. Identify ways to "process [a] responsible, healthy theological exploration" of the spiritual quest.

16. If we were to create a climate in the church that encourages and supports engagement in spiritual practice, what would it look and feel like? How would it affect your congregation and its contact with the community?

Healing through Hospitality

One cold morning in 1981, a business commuter named Karen Olson was moved to purchase a sandwich for a homeless woman she saw huddled in a threadbare coat on the streets of New York. She planned to just toss the sandwich and move on, but the woman caught her hand, and they began a conversation. Karen realized that, almost more than the food, this woman craved some meaningful contact with another human being. She later shared the story with her sons, and they began traveling every weekend from their home in New Jersey to the streets of New York to distribute sack lunches and talk with people forced to live on the streets. She began to learn about homelessness and eventually, with the help of several congregations and synagogues, established an organization now known as the National Interfaith Hospitality Network.[48] Initially, ten faith communities agreed to provide temporary shelter for families on a rotating basis so that each congregation housed families for one week out of each ten, with members volunteering to spend the evenings with the families playing games, talking, helping to care for children, cooking meals, and preparing sack lunches for the following day. The movement continues to grow and now there are networks operating or developing in more than twenty states.

17. Why is this a story about healing of the spirit? There are also elements of sharing in this story. Talk about the connections between sharing and healing of the spirit. Discuss how this story also illustrates other disciplines.

Conclusion

To walk the path of the disciple takes us to the mountaintop or into the forest or alongside the oceans in search of the God who resides within our own souls. From our beginnings, "we declared that God is not closed up in a box or a book, but that the Spirit wanders freely across the geography of our lives so as to find its way into our hearts."[49] Are we willing to free God to work as God will in our lives and our world?

Closing

Sing together "God of the Sparrow," *Sing for Peace* (*SP* 13), and close with prayer focused on the call to spiritual quest.

Chapter 6

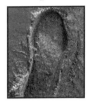

Stand
for Justice

Key Scripture

Become a people of the Temple—those who see violence but proclaim peace, who feel conflict yet extend the hand of reconciliation, who encounter broken spirits and find pathways for healing.

Fulfill the purposes of the Temple by making its ministries manifest in your hearts. It was built from your sacrifices and searching over many generations. Let it stand as a towering symbol of a people who knew injustice and strife on the frontier and who now seek the peace of Jesus Christ throughout the world.

—Doctrine and Covenants 161:2a–b

1. Brainstorm and list for the class any words that come to mind when you say the word "justice." What questions or thoughts come to mind when the topic of justice comes up? What are you seeking to understand in this area?

A Call to Discipleship—Grant McMurray[50]

Sixth, the path of the disciple requires us to stand up for justice. If we are to be faithful, we will become courageous witnesses of the call to stand for the dispossessed, to declare love where there is violence, to speak healing where there is estrangement, and to join with God in the journey toward the peaceable kingdom, where the unity of all creation is honored and celebrated.

When we speak of such things we usually think of the big issues of the world, of the struggle to overcome discriminations

71

against people on the basis of race or creed, sexual orientation or gender, tribe or nationality. The question is joined at the point where power meets faith and where the dreams of our hearts are matched to the realities of our age.

But I want to suggest that justice-making is not just about those questions but also about the things we encounter every day in our congregations. David Schaal, the pastor of the Stone Church [in April 2000], has received permission from those involved so that I might share the following story. It may have some sensitive elements for them, but it is the real life of the church as it transforms the people whom it encounters.

April and Randy are teenage sister and brother. One year ago, they were living with their mother in a small Midwestern town. Without going into great personal detail, suffice it to say that their lives were very difficult and lacked the love, affirmation, and personal care that all of God's children deserve. In response to their circumstance they reacted in ways that reflected the frustration and loneliness of their hearts. Randy dropped out of high school; April left home and spent a year "on the street."

After a while, when their hearts' yearning for a place to call home intensified, they moved to Independence to live with their father and stepmother. In this new home they found safety, discipline, and love. Much to their surprise, they also found something else that would significantly change their lives. Their father and stepmother introduced them to a new group of friends—a youth group at the Stone Church.

In the fellowship of the senior high group, for the first time they found friends who cared *for* them, not for what they could get *from* them. Sensitive youth leaders listened to their stories, their concerns, their fears, and chatted with them about Jesus, about the church, and about how pleased they were that April and Randy had come to be a part of the group. Other Saints surrounded them with care and kindness. April is no longer on the street but in a home and a congregation where she and her brother are loved. Randy is back in school and working hard.

April was baptized about six weeks ago. Randy was baptized two weeks later. Following one of the baptismal services, this delightful brother and sister embraced, and with broad smiles said to one another, "I can hardly believe how our lives have changed in just one year!"

Equally exciting is that both of them have voiced their desire to share their story with other teens and adults, hoping that their experience can be helpful to someone else. It is apparent that their lives are being transformed, because their concern is already being directed outward to others in need of their witness.

There is nothing extraordinary about this story, except for the fact that two lost kids were found, that a few ordinary folks joined together to demonstrate their love and care, and that this business of transformation isn't finally about numbers. It is about lives of people made whole because somebody had the courage to say: "This isn't fair. This isn't right. This isn't just."

2. As you look at the people in your congregation, neighborhood, relatives, friends, and community, what kinds of peace and justice issues do you see? Which ones do you get most excited about?

3. Share any stories that you know (and would not be breaking confidences to tell) that show the impact of the gospel in situations needing justice.

Scripture Study

What does the LORD require of you but to do justice, and to love kindness, and to walk humbly with your God?

—Micah 6:8

Let justice roll down like waters.

—Amos 5:24

Justice, and only justice, you shall pursue.

—Deuteronomy 16:20

4. So what is justice? Clearly, we are required to do it, to pursue it, and to let it flow, so how do we know what it is? One constantly hears the line (sometimes as a whine) "It isn't fair!" Are justice and fairness the same thing? As you think about justice and fairness, remember the parable from Matthew about

73

the workers in the vineyard who were paid the same whether they worked all day or for just a short while (Matthew 20:1–16). Was such a a payment system fair? Was it just? Support your opinion.

> *You who are my disciples must be found continuing in the forefront of those organizations and movements which are recognizing the worth of persons and are committed to bringing the ministry of my Son to bear on their lives.*
> —Doctrine and Covenants 151:9

> *You shall not deprive a resident alien or an orphan of justice; you shall not take a widow's garment in pledge. Remember that you were a slave in Egypt and the LORD your God redeemed you from there…. When you reap your harvest in your field and forget a sheaf in the field, you shall not go back to get it; it shall be left for the alien, the orphan, and the widow, so that the LORD your God may bless you in all your undertakings. When you beat your olive trees, do not strip what is left; it shall be for the alien, the orphan, and the widow. When you gather the grapes of your vineyard, do not glean what is left; it shall be for the alien, the orphan, and the widow. Remember that you were a slave in the land of Egypt.*
> —Deuteronomy 24:17–22

5. All people are of worth and should be treated as children of God. By reminding the Jews that they were slaves in Egypt, God reminded them that they were once the less fortunate, the downtrodden. It is reminiscent of the common comment, "There but for the grace of God, go I." Someone once said, "Fairness is treating everyone the same, while justice is treating everyone the way you hope they would treat you, if the tables were turned." What truth do you see in that statement?

Exploring Standing for Justice as Active Participants—
Larry McGuire[51]

For me, it is simply not enough to say I will stand for justice. I believe I must not only be an advocate of justice, but I must also be an active participant in confronting and dismantling the causes of injustice. Sometimes that has caused me to confront the injustice in our society which, in reality, is easy to do. However, what am I to do when the injustice is taking place within the institution that employs me? What if the injustice I confront is taking

74

place within a congregation in my jurisdiction, and those being confronted demand I be removed and sent elsewhere?

When I consider Grant McMurray's call of the path of the disciple to include the ideal and practice of justice, I find myself asking, whose justice? What are the qualities that I believe justice must have in order for it to be true justice? What will this require of me and of ministers of Jesus Christ?

The first question of "whose justice" is basic as long as we agree it is God's justice. As long as our views of God's justice are the same, we can easily agree that it is God's justice we seek to uphold, embrace, and live out. Walter Brueggemann commented in the book *Theology of the Old Testament*:

> **From the outset, Yahweh is known to be a God committed to the establishment of concrete, sociopolitical justice in a world of massive power organized against justice. It is voiced suffering that sets in motion Yahweh's uncompromising resolve for the transformation of earthly power arrangements.**[52]

Brueggemann went on to discuss the idea of distributive justice, which is the inequity of the distribution of the goods and power of Israel's day, and the idea of retributive justice or a system of rewards and punishments, "giving to persons what is their just desert on the basis of performance."[53]

Micah 6:8 is a very popular scripture to use when we want to make the point that we believe in justice. *"He has told you, O mortal, what is good; and what does the LORD require of you but to do justice, and to love kindness, and to walk humbly with your God?"* Notice, it is to **do justice.** It is not enough to believe in it. It is not enough to aspire to just living or just conditions. The requirement is to do justice. The expectation is that the people of God will be the ones doing the dismantling of injustice and be the restorers of righteous living.

Now to my second question, what are the qualities of justice? The ideals of Transformation 2000 called the church to some incredible expectations. From my perspective, the element that has received the greatest attention is the practice of reconciliation. I believe this is an element of justice. However, it is not the end-all that I sometimes think we have focused on at the expense of some other critical areas.

In order for us to truly be a people practicing and doing justice, we must address issues of power. Such issues include power over people and the reality that in order for us to be ambassadors of justice we must continue to dismantle the pockets of power that still exist in our congregations, our districts, yes, even in our headquarters structure. Along with the issue of dismantling power comes the idea of integrity. For me, we must always operate with the highest degree of integrity. We cannot allow pockets of negotiated injustice to occur. When we allow that, we dismantle the integrity of justice. Integrity must always be blanketed in compassion and respect. Compassion for people and respect for their situation must always be our guide.

So what does this require of me? As I prepared to share these thoughts, I realized that my experience of working in Chicago gave me numerous examples I could recite. Each one caused me to confront my own biases and the biases of the church. My experience with Homeless On the Move for Equality—an organization dedicated to empowering those experiencing the reality of homelessness through training and advocacy—was the first thing I recalled. They asked me to serve as their honorary "homee" and pastor. One time they invited me to experience homelessness firsthand by being with them overnight on the streets of Chicago. It was one of the most frightening and humiliating experiences I have ever encountered. I was deloused with flea powder, my clothes were run through the same procedure, I was given a worn sheet to sleep on and rousted out by 5:30 a.m. to hear some preacher condemn my ways of sin before I could have my breakfast. I experienced going to federal court to be a part of a lawsuit to prohibit the city of Chicago from gathering the belongings of the individuals living along Lower Wacker Drive and throwing those belongings in the dump without any compensation to the people.

Today my role is different, and I am on a new journey to experience the doing of justice. I don't know how I will be a doer, but I pray it will be with compassion, respect, integrity, and the spirit of reconciliation.

In the 1995 movie *Crimson Tide*, Gene Hackman argued with his second-in-command about a decision that had been made.

Hackman declared, "We're here to preserve democracy, not practice it." I pray that will not be the case for us as we walk the path of the disciple. We must be doers of justice, not simply preservers of some ideal.

6. Why does a situation sometimes feel like justice to one person or group but not to another? Share some examples.

7. What stands in the way of justice in society? in your own life?

8. What are the qualities of justice? Draw up guidelines or standards to guide people in justice-making practices.

Justice for the Workers—Jane Gardner

In 1929, manufacturing companies were not only a source of employment, but they also provided housing, food, gas, clothing, and other necessary items for their employees. When Ezra Cooper went to work for a company, he discovered that, while the executives made big money, the laborers were not paid an adequate wage. In addition, most of the employees had large charge balances with the company for their daily needs with no hope of ever paying off the debt. The workers started before daylight and did not go home until after dark—six days a week, no overtime, no holidays, no paid vacation, and most importantly, no representation. If workers were treated unfairly, they had nowhere to turn.

Cooper had grown up in an area without any modern conveniences—dirt roads, no running water or electricity. He believed that people should help each other. It was unthinkable to him that anyone, even a company, would treat people the way these workers were being treated. So in 1937, he became very involved in union organization at the plant.

The company was opposed to organized labor. In 1938, Cooper, as a leader among the workers, supported the union as it called for a strike. Acceptable working conditions and fair wages were the key issues behind the strike. The situation soon turned ugly. Cooper and a group of employees took over the plant and refused to let anybody in. They turned law enforcement officers away and locked out company officials for eight days. Finally the governor ordered the militia to move in and end the lockout. As martial law was enforced, Cooper and his co-workers peacefully ended their occupation, leaving the plant, which was surrounded by uniformed soldiers carrying bayonet rifles. Many people were arrested that day including most of the employees considered to be troublemakers.

Because of this experience, Cooper spent the next forty years working through the union to improve working conditions and wages. He was quoted as saying, "I don't hate the company, and I don't want to break them because they furnish jobs. I just want to see the people treated fairly and receiving a living wage."

Cooper held many positions in the union (line steward, shop steward, and executive board member), but he is most remembered for his leadership and commitment to justice for the plant workers.

9. Describe the situation in this story from the owner's viewpoint. Then describe the situation from the workers' viewpoint. What elements would the owner and workers agree on when trying to work out a solution? Discuss the advantages of being able to look at a situation from more than one perspective.

10. What principles should guide people like Ezra Cooper and us in situations that might need changing?

Alexander Doniphan Disobeys[54]

In 1838, Joseph Smith Jr., Sidney Rigdon, Hyrum Smith, Lyman Wight, Parley P. Pratt, George W. Robinson, and Amasa Lyman were tried and convicted by a military court martial of treason and sentenced to be executed by a firing squad. Alexander Doniphan was a Liberty, Missouri, lawyer whose militia unit had been called into active duty to respond to the "Mormon rebellion." Doniphan had protested that the entire proceeding was illegal. In the end, Doniphan, as the militia commander, was ordered to carry out the court-martial's sentence. Doniphan refused to carry out the order and responded in writing to his commander, "It is cold-blooded murder. I will not obey your order. My brigade shall march for Liberty tomorrow morning, at 8 o'clock; and if you execute these men, I will hold you responsible before an earthly tribunal, so help me God."[55] In the face of Doniphan's firm stand, others in command did not carry out the death sentences.

11. Civil disobedience is a touchy subject. It might be easy for us to applaud Doniphan's refusal to shoot Joseph Smith, but do we feel equally supportive of people who choose to disobey a law we think seems reasonable or even necessary? How do we make the determination whether a person's act is one of civil disobedience that merits condemnation or one of "divine obedience" that merits our support?

12. Divide the class into groups representing the following viewpoints of how to solve peace and justice issues:
    preaching and teaching the gospel
    using participatory community development
    using charity and welfare
    advocating through political action to change systems and
        policies
Name a situation in which peace and justice is needed and with which everyone is familiar. The class will try to decide what action should be taken with everyone arguing from the viewpoint of their own group's view. When finished, discuss the experience and summarize what the class learned. What other viewpoints could have been included?

At What Cost?

There are many stories of people who have been willing to give their lives for a just cause. Late in the fourth century, a monk named Telemachus was stirred by the Spirit of God to leave his desert home and confront the evil of gladiators killing one another in Rome. Once there, before a roaring crowd of thousands waiting to see the butchery, Telemachus leaped across a retaining wall and ran into the arena, placing himself between two warriors. Though his presence at first startled the fighters and onlookers alike, the mob soon began shouting for the gladiators to kill the monk who was hindering their fun. Finally the commander of the games gave his nod, and with a flash of one of the gladiators' swords, Telemachus was struck dead. The crowd fell silent. Stunned by the horror their savage instincts had wrought, the crowd began to leave the arena. On that day, the horrible games ended, never to be revived.[56]

13. Can you think of other examples of people who have been willing to die for their beliefs?

14. Think of the story of the village of Le Chambon used earlier in this text. In what ways does that story speak to you of the call to stand for justice? Choose one story from each of the various sections of this text. Talk about each story from the perspective of another of the disciplines other than the one it was used to illustrate.

Justice: Becoming Whole or Getting Even?

Many people live in cultures that often equate justice with punishment of wrongdoing. "Justice" is a system for making sure those who commit crimes or other wrongs "pay" for what they have done. Such retributive systems ask three essential questions: (1) What laws have been broken? (2) Who broke the law? (3) What shall we do to punish the lawbreaker?

More and more there are discussions of a different approach to justice. Restorative justice approaches violence in its many forms from another perspective. It asks different questions in an effort to discover how to make victims of crime, offenders, and their communities whole again. Restorative justice asks: (1) Who has been hurt? (2) What are their needs? (3) Whose obligations are these needs?

There are many models emerging that use a restorative justice approach. In some native cultures, there is a long tradition of restorative justice worked out through tribal or community councils or circles that seek ways to restore health to the entire community after there has been a breach of trust between two or more of its members. There are victim offender mediation programs in many communities. There seems to be a growing awareness that while punishment can be relatively swift and simple, it is not always effective.

15. How might it change an approach to crime to ask the questions posed by restorative justice?

16. Think of a situation you have read about or heard about in your community in which someone was accused of breaking the law. Think of ways the situation might be addressed from a restorative justice model. If we begin by using restorative jus-

tice in simple, everyday differences, we will become more adept at it and will be better able to apply it to the more difficult situations we encounter in life.

Wholeness for All through New Vision of Self for One—
Sherrie Taylor and Ray Taylor[57]

In the South African Babemba tribe, when a person commits a crime or acts unjustly, she or he is brought to the center of the village, unbound and alone. Every man, woman, and child in the village ceases all work and gathers in a large circle around the person who has acted irresponsibly. Each person talks out loud to the accused person about all the good things the accused has done in his or her lifetime. Every experience and every incident that can be remembered is recounted with as much accuracy and detail as possible. All of the person's positive characteristics, attributes, strengths, good deeds, and acts of kindness are retold at length and with great care. No one is permitted to exaggerate or fabricate or be facetious. This tribal ceremony sometimes goes on for days, and it does not end until everyone is drained of positive comments about the wrongdoer. At the end, the accused person is literally and symbolically welcomed back into the community. A joyous celebration takes place. The incident of wrongdoing is never again mentioned.

17. Many experts tell us the best way to ensure good behavior from young children is not to punish their mistakes but to praise their successes—help them create a positive image of themselves that they will strive to live up to. The Babemba tribe's system of justice strives to help a person who has acted irresponsibly see a new and more positive vision of themselves. Discuss ways this idea might be effectively incorporated into dealing with hurtful or irresponsible behaviors.

18. We are familiar with the story of the prodigal son (Luke 15:11–32). What similarities to that story do you see in this system of justice?

Conclusion

To walk the path of the disciple, we must stand up for justice. "We endured the oppression and violence of the mobs and then

81

adopted a church seal that placed the lion, the lamb, and the little child in a peaceful circle of love."[58] How will we be courageous and outspoken in our witness against those forces of injustice we encounter?

Closing

Sing together "This We Can Do," *Sing for Peace* (*SP* 32), and close with prayer focused on the call to stand for justice.

Notes

1. *Saints Herald* 144 (August 1997): 315.
2. Ibid.
3. W. Grant McMurray, "A Transforming Faith: A Call to Discipleship," *Saints Herald* 147 (June 2000): 183–191.
4. Ibid., 186.
5. M. Scott Peck, *The Different Drum: Community-Making and Peace* (New York: Simon and Schuster, 1987), 86–106.
6. Ibid., 106.
7. Ken Barrows, "Anxiously Engaged," an unpublished paper presented at the Field Officers Meeting, September 11, 2000.
8. Robert P. Bruch, "These Are the Times, We Are the People" *Outreach* (Winter/Spring 1990): 3.
9. Philip P. Hallie, *Lest Innocent Blood Be Shed: The Story of the Village of Le Chambon and How Goodness Happened There* (New York: Harper & Row, 1979).
10. Ibid., 12.
11. McMurray, 190.
12. McMurray, 186–187.
13. Wallace B. Smith, "Exiles in Time," *Saints Herald* 139 (April 1992): 137.
14. Mary Jacks Dynes, "Reconciliation and the Dance of Being Female," unpublished paper presented at the Field Officers Meeting, September 11, 2000.
15. Sue Monk Kidd, *The Dance of the Dissident Daughter: A Woman's Journey from Christian Tradition to the Sacred Feminine* (San Francisco: HarperSanFrancisco, 1996), 57.
16. Suzanne Zuecher, *The Enneagram: Personality and Prayer* (audiocassette from Credence Communications, 2000).
17. Kidd, 49.
18. Ibid., 59.
19. Carlo Carretto, *The God Who Comes*, Rose Mary Hancock, trans. (Maryknoll, New York: Orbis Books, 1974), 183.
20. Rosemary Radford Ruether, *Women and Redemption: A Theological History* (Minneapolis: Fortress Press, 1998), 279.
21. Elizabeth A. Johnson, *She Who Is: The Mystery of God in Feminist Theological Discourse* (New York: Crossroad Publishing

Company, 1992), 27.

22. Johnson, 4.
23. Kidd, 153.
24. Ibid., 227.
25. Danny A. Belrose, "Homecoming: Reflections on Rembrandt's *Return of the Prodigal Son*," presented at the Pacific Northwest Evangelists/Teachers Gathering, Portland, Oregon, September 24, 2000.
26. McMurray, 190.
27. Ibid., 187.
28. Matthew 14: 13–21, Mark 6: 30–44, Luke 9: 10–17, John 6: 1–13.
29. Dave Nii, "The Path of the Disciple Is to Share Willingly from the Blessings of Our Lives: Personal Reflection," unpublished paper presented at the Field Officers Meeting, September 11, 2000.
30. Dolores LaChapelle from *Earth Festivals* by Delores LaChapelle and Janet Bourque, Finn Hill Arts Publishers. Silverton, Colorado, 1973. Used by permission of the author.
31. As told by Gregg McDonald, "Tell the Good News," a sermon delivered April 7, 2000, at World Conference.
32. Jeff Brumbeau, *The Quiltmaker's Gift*, pictures by Gail de Marcken (Duluth, Minnesota: Pfeifer-Hamilton Publishers, 2000).
33. McMurray, 190.
34. Ibid., 187–188.
35. Francis W. Kelley, "Learning: An Expanded Reflection," unpublished paper presented at the Field Officers Meeting, September 11, 2000.
36. Aristotle, *Metaphysics* (Ann Arbor: University of Michigan Press, 1952), Book Alpha, Line I, adapted.
37. Galileo, quoted in James L. Christian, *Philosophy: An Introduction to the Art of Wondering* (New York: Holt, Rinehart, and Winston, 1986), 24.
38. Eartha Kitt, quoted in *A Little Learning Is a Dangerous Thing*, James Charlton, ed.(New York: St. Martin's Press, 1994), 109.

39. B. R. Hergenhahn, *An Introduction to Theories of Learning*, 3rd ed. (Englewood Cliffs, New Jersey: Prentice Hall, 1988), 7. Cited in Sharan B. Merriam and Rosemary S. Caffarella, *Learning in Adulthood: A Comprehensive Guide* (San Francisco: Jossey-Bass Publishers, 1991), 124.
40. Václav Havel, "The Need for Transcendence in the Postmodern World," *The Futurist* 29 (July/August 1995): 142.
41. Eduard C. Lindeman, *The Meaning of Adult Education* (Montreal: Harvest House, 1961), xxvii.
42. Paul Alan Laughlin and Glenna S. Jackson, *Remedial Christianity: What Every Believer Should Know about the Faith, but Probably Doesn't* (Santa Rosa, California: Polebridge Press, 2000), 11.
43. Ibid., 16.
44. Ibid.
45. McMurray, 190.
46. Ibid., 188–189.
47. David Schaal, "Spirituality and the Church: Reflections on the Path Ahead," unpublished paper presented at Field Officers Meeting, September 11, 2000.
48. For more information see *www.nihn.org* or call 908/273-1100.
49. McMurray, 190.
50. Ibid., 189.
51. Larry McGuire, "Reaction to Sixth Path of the Disciple: Justice," unpublished paper presented at the Field Officers Meeting, September 11, 2000.
52. Walter Brueggemann, *Theology of the Old Testament: Testimony, Dispute, Advocacy* (Minneapolis: Fortress Press, 1997), 736.
53. Ibid., 737.
54. Roger D. Launius, "Alexander William Doniphan and the 1838 Mormon War in Missouri," *The John Whitmer Historical Association Journal* 18 (1998): 81–101.
55. *History of Caldwell and Livingston Counties, Missouri* (St. Louis: National Historical Co., 1886), 137. Quoted in Launius, 92.

56. Robert B. Setzer Jr., *Encounters with the Living Christ: Meeting Jesus in the Gospel of John* (Valley Forge, Pennsylvania: Judson Press 1999), 98–99, citing William Barclay, *The Gospel of Mark* (Philadelphia: Westminster Press, 1975), 204–205.

57. Sherrie Taylor and Ray Taylor, "Restorative Justice as an Alternative to the Death Penalty: A Christian Moral Perspective to Human Rights," presented at 2000 Peace Colloquy, Independence, Missouri. Story about Babemba tribe told at *www.humankindness.org/Winter 98.html*.

58. McMurray, 190.

Appendix A

President W. Grant McMurray submitted the following counsel to the quorums, councils, and orders of the church and to the World Conference on Tuesday, April 4, 2000. Conference delegates voted on April 7, 2000, to include this document in the Doctrine and Covenants. President McMurray prefaced his "Words of Counsel to the Church" with the following introductory statement:

"On April 21, 1996, I brought to the church words of counsel which I felt led to share, without any specific instruction as to their ultimate disposition. I felt it was important that the church live with the words and not feel compelled to make any urgent decisions about them. During the intervening four years I have been led back to them many times and have pondered their meaning and their timeliness. Without clinging to every word or phrase, I have remained assured of the rightness of the message, but I have also sensed that it was incomplete, that there was more to be said. I did not then understand that our journey of transformation would instill new depth and insight.

"I have continued to wrestle with the message, sensitive to the importance of expressing it with integrity and always aware of my own human failings and uncertainties. In accordance with the responsibilities I carry, filled with love for the church and its people, and grateful to a God who sustains me in my many weaknesses, I humbly present the following counsel to the church for whatever formal consideration may be appropriate. I do so confident that the Spirit which accompanied its preparation will also abide with those who embrace its challenge."

To the Councils, Quorums, and Orders, to the World Conference, and to the Church:

1a. Lift up your eyes and fix them on the place beyond the horizon to which you are sent. Journey in trust, assured that the great and marvelous work is for this time and for all time.

b. Claim your unique and sacred place within the circle of those who call upon the name of Jesus Christ. Be faithful to the spirit of the Restoration, mindful that it is a spirit of adventure, openness, and searching. Walk proudly and with a quickened step. Be a joyful people. Laugh and play and sing, embodying the hope and freedom of the gospel.

2a. Become a people of the Temple–those who see violence but proclaim peace, who feel conflict yet extend the hand of reconciliation, who encounter broken spirits and find pathways for healing.

b. Fulfill the purposes of the Temple by making its ministries manifest in your hearts. It was built from your sacrifices and searching over many generations. Let it stand as a towering symbol of a people who knew injustice and strife on the frontier and who now seek the peace of Jesus Christ throughout the world.

3a. Open your hearts and feel the yearnings of your brothers and sisters who are lonely, despised, fearful, neglected, unloved. Reach out in understanding, clasp their hands, and invite all to share in the blessings of community created in the name of the One who suffered on behalf of all.

b. Do not be fearful of one another. Respect each life journey, even in its brokenness and uncertainty, for each person has walked alone at times. Be ready to listen and slow to criticize, lest judgments be unrighteous and unredemptive.

c. Be patient with one another, for creating sacred community is arduous and even painful. But it is to loving community such as this that each is called. Be courageous and visionary, believing in the power of just a few vibrant witnesses to transform the world. Be assured that love will overcome the voices of fear, division, and deceit.

d. Understand that the road to transformation travels both inward and outward. The road to transformation is the path of the disciple.

4a. Do not neglect the smallest among you, for even the least of these are treasures in God's sight. Receive the giftedness and energy of children and youth, listening to understand their questions and their wisdom. Respond to their need to be loved and nurtured as they grow.

b. Be mindful of the changing of life's seasons, of the passage from the springtime of childhood and youth to the winter years of life. Embrace the blessing of your many differences. Be tender and caring. Be reminded once again that the gifts of all are necessary in order that divine purposes may be accomplished.

5 Be respectful of tradition. Do not fail to listen attentively to the telling of the sacred story, for the story of scripture and of faith empowers and illuminates. But neither be captive to time-bound formulas and procedures. Remember that instruction given in former years is applicable in principle and must be measured against the needs of a growing church, in accordance with the prayerful direction of the spiritual authorities and the consent of the people.

6a. Stand firm in the name of the One you proclaim and create diverse communities of disciples and seekers, rejoicing in the continuing fulfillment of the call to this people to prophetically witness in the name of Jesus Christ.

b. Heed the urgent call to become a global family united in the name of the Christ, committed in love to one another, seeking the kingdom for which you yearn and to which you have always been summoned. That kingdom shall be a peaceable one and it shall be known as Zion.

7 The Spirit of the One you follow is the spirit of love and peace. That Spirit seeks to abide in the hearts of those who would embrace its call and live its message. The path will not always be easy, the choices will not always be clear, but the cause is sure and the Spirit will bear witness to the truth, and those who live the truth will know the hope and the joy of discipleship in the community of Christ. Amen.

W. Grant McMurray
President of the Church

INDEPENDENCE, MISSOURI
APRIL 4, 2000

A Transforming Faith: A Call to Discipleship

World Conference Monday evening address, April 3, 2000

By W. Grant McMurray

A few months ago I had opportunity to travel throughout the Orient, and one Sunday morning I found myself in the Seoul, Korea, congregation. As I was visiting with the Saints before the service, I was introduced to a young man who was a visitor to the congregation. He said he was a Mormon and had been investigating our church through his contact with Steve Shields, our appointee minister assigned to Korea. He was inquisitive and thoughtful in his statements to me.

After the service, I was again visiting and the man approached me.

"I am very privileged to meet you," he said. "You are a very humble man. You stand and talk to all of the people. You are a very humble man." I muttered my thanks and indicated that that was the way we did things in our church.

"You are a very humble man," he continued. "You get down on the floor and play with the children and laugh with them. You are a very humble man." I assured him that I enjoyed playing with children and that it wasn't hard duty at all for me, and thanked him for his words.

"You are a very humble man," he persisted. And pointing to my wrist he said, "You wear a cheap watch. You are a very humble man." Between slightly gritted teeth, I indicated that we believed in good stewardship and didn't want to be extravagant in any way.

"You are a very humble man," he reiterated, now for the fourth time. "You wear a cheap coat and cheap slacks." By this time I felt I had received quite enough testimonies to my humility. I moved on.

I shared this experience with my family when I returned home and at Christmas got a nice Seiko watch out of the deal. My wardrobe is still a little threadbare, though, so if you want to assist, you may bring your castoffs and deposit them in the large baskets we've placed in the Temple reception hall.

That story is ringing in my ears as I say to you in absolute candor that I come to you tonight in all humility. It is a daunting task to stand at the bridge to a new millennium and speak about the future of the church I love. To speak truth to such a moment is to lay down the barriers of conventionality and be willing to press against the boundaries of possibility. To speak truth to such a moment is to be willing to both embrace the incredible energy and excitement of our gathering and what we have ac-complished together and at the same time to proclaim soberly that it is not enough, that the future demands something from us that is deeper, more risky, more challenging than any celebration will allow.

I showed someone around the Temple Lot the other day, driving its perimeters and trying to explain the significance of this plot of ground. To see it in today's splendor obscures what it once was. Just imagine what this piece of land was like in 1831 when Joseph Smith Jr. somehow found his way to this place at the very edge of the frontier, stumbled through the brush, and marked the spot where the Temple should be built. We were a brand-new church struggling for our very existence, led by a brash and controversial prophet with a few zealous followers and a formidable array of detractors. What audacity to stand on such a place and declare it to be a land of promise and the "Center Place of Zion."

As I drove the boundaries of the land, I was struck by how difficult it was to explain what it all means to us. In a complex way, its meaning is a unique blend of ancient and archaic images with powerful, contemporary meanings. The sections of the Doctrine and Covenants that define it use terms that most people of the twenty-first century no longer use, phrases that we rarely preach about, concepts that are completely reinterpreted, if we use them at all.

And yet, the imagery is inescapable—for those of us birthed into this movement it is the language of our childhood, of our religious faith, of our own deeply personal quest for meaning and purpose in our lives. Somehow, standing on the brink of a new millennium, it is critically important for us to both capture the profound faith journey of those who went before us and at the same time be radically open to the discovery of what God would have us do, of what kind of people we are truly called to be. In that regard, there is no more powerful linking image from our tradition than the Temple we built from out of our faith and heritage, not even being sure what we would do it with it once we had it.

For the past three years our church has been engaged in an exciting journey to create a meaningful future for our movement and to embrace a mission worthy of our heritage

and our people. To engage in such an endeavor was an act of faith, not only in the future but in the belief that God is with us. In some respects it was to reflect together about what kind of people we wanted to be and then to declare that we would be that kind of people.

The response of the church to Transformation 2000 has been a heartening tribute to the historic capacity of this movement to be resilient and to adapt. Perhaps our people truly are inheritors of the Restoration principle that essentially calls us to reshape the mission of the church to fit the times in which it is expressed. It calls us away from a theology of fear that hunkers down because the future is uncertain and at times distasteful. Instead, it calls us into engagement with the forces of culture, shaping rather than denying it, connecting with it rather than building a fortress to protect us from it.

I sense within you just the beginnings of an awareness of what that might mean. Our people have always been uncomfortable with trying to be like every other church. That is why they strove so mightily against ecumenism for so long.

We have always been taught that we are different, that we have something unique to offer the world. The fundamentalist backlash of the past few decades within the church has come from two things: fear of changing those eternal verities that have been the hallmark of our faith and resistance to cultural adaptation that seemed to make us just like everyone else. The first is a very conservative principle and the second is a radical positioning of the movement over against the culture.

In Transformation 2000 we leaned against both of those principles. We embraced change, not begrudgingly but enthusiastically, arguing that we *must* be transformed if we are to fulfill our mission. At the same time, we embraced our story and declared that indeed we *are* different and we do have something unique to contribute. In the process we recast that story so as to discover the mythic truths that lay shimmering at its core. From out of persecution and rejection we discovered peace and reconciliation. From out of exclusive, gathered American communitarian experiments we discovered inclusive global community. From out of a ritualistic temple cultus we discovered an expansive, symbolic, and sacramental understanding of temple theology.

Leonard Sweet, a cutting-edge writer who focuses on the new spiritual meanderings in the world today, speaks to the tidal waves of change that are the aftermath of the postmodern earthquake. He puts his challenge to the church in this way:

> Can the church stop its puny, hack dreams of trying to "make a difference in the world" and start dreaming God-sized dreams of making the world different? Can the church help invent and prevent, redeem and redream, this post-modern future? If the future ain't what it used to be, as the great philosopher Yogi Berra once said, can the church make the future what God wants it to be?
> —*SoulTsunami: Sink or Swim in New Millenium Culture*, p. 16

I believe our people are ready to be challenged anew and to engage in the struggle to create a vision of the kingdom of God on earth, which is, after all, what our church has always been about. Part of the appeal of Transformation 2000 was that we gave precedence to the dream over the barriers and, as a result, achieved far more than practical scheming ever would have allowed. That foolish faith called us to be better than we had ever been, to dream bigger dreams and to truly believe the words we mouth, and the hymns we sing, and the prayers we pray. And we discovered that our foolishness was not so foolish after all.

Perhaps you remember the eerie and mystical story that surfaced in the months after the Temple design was announced. That design was conceived by the Japanese architect Gyo Obata after the concept of the chambered nautilus, often popularly described as a shell. When the first renderings of the design were published in the *Herald* it caused quite a stir among a group of women in their seventies and eighties. Their minds went back more than sixty years to when they participated in an organization for young women of the church. It was called Temple Builders. What stunned them was that the logo they had adopted as symbolic of their organization was the nautilus shell, the very design that emerged a half century later in the mind of an architect who didn't even know of their existence. The pin they used to signify membership was the nautilus shape with the letters "TB" (Temple Builders) engraved upon it.

Alice May Burgess authored the sixty-seven-page handbook in 1920. It was called *Temple Builders Book: A Manual of Instruction and Suggestions for Temple Builders.* She wrote the following:

> Our symbol is nature's most famous builder, the pearly nautilus. This little sea animal patiently constructs its own house, and each year sees the addition of a beautiful new room into which the nautilus moves, leaving behind, and walling up, the old quarters...So we must build, patiently, unremittingly, making beautiful our materials, erecting from what life brings to us a pure white structure, well-balanced, symmetrical—the temple of our souls.... What are you building, girls? A temple with spires pointing heavenward, or a hovel, hugging the ground? —As told in "Temple Builders: 1918 and 1989," by Barbara Howard, *Saints Herald*, February 1989, pp. 11–12, 22.

As young women joined the chapters of the Temple Builders they learned to recite Oliver Wendell Holmes's poem, "The Chambered Nautilus." The poet speaks of the "ship of pearl" that "poets feign" and points to the chambered cells "where its dim dreaming life was wont to dwell," and then he describes its growth and change:

Year after year beheld the silent toil
That spread his lustrous coil;
Still, as the spiral grew,
He left the past year's dwelling for the new,
Stole with soft step its shining archway through,
Built up its idle door,
Stretched in his last-found home, and knew the old no more.

It is a concept reminiscent of II Corinthians 5:17 in which we are told: "So if anyone is in Christ, there is a new creation: everything old has passed away; see, everything has become new!"(NRSV). There is a profound and meaningful tension between being an inheritor of our chambered cells, grateful for their essential nurture, and being a new creation stretching beyond the "last-found home" and knowing "the old no more."

It is time to reflect with absolute honesty on the journey before us. At the end of the Transformation 2000 address three years ago I spoke of the need to follow the courageous example of Jesus, who rode "into the very heart of his own fears on a road strewn with palms." That triumphal entry into Jerusalem, I remind you, is viewed by us from the perspective of those who know how it turned out—through the victory of Easter. But Palm Sunday was a day in which the future was not known. In Luke 19 we are told what Jesus experienced in that moment outside Jerusalem: "As he came near and saw the city, he wept over it, saying, 'If you, even you, had only recognized on this day the things that make for peace! But now they are hidden from your eyes'"(Luke 19:41–42 NRSV). I pray that the day will not come when it can be said of our faith that we had a chance to know the things that make for peace but failed to recognize what it took, and now those things are hidden from our eyes.

Tonight, we summon the church to a transforming faith that moves us prophetically into the future, not knowing where our journey might take us, but assured that we are led by the God who birthed this people on the frontier and now leads us toward the peaceable kingdom, which we call Zion. We are called to be disciples, to follow Jesus Christ. It is he who makes for peace, who reconciles, and heals. It is for us to discern what such a call means in a world that is not at peace and where people are separated and broken and lost.

This call to the church grows out of the heart of our sacred journey. But now we are asked to go deeper, to go beyond the words that touch the imagination so as to encounter the Spirit, which compels the response. It is to take the sometimes long pathway from the mind to the heart, connecting the two in an unbroken thread of knowing and doing. It is to lay aside predispositions and tired bromides that soothe but do not inspire, and instead to take up the cross and walk the path of the disciple. And here is where we must go.

Community

First, the path of the disciple calls us to community. The people who built a teeming city of followers on the banks of the Mississippi are now called to build a diverse community of disciples from the farthest corners of the world. We will be a community that invites and embraces all those desiring a home in the body of Christ, including male and female, young and old, rich and poor, and people of all races, cultures, and life experiences.

With the model of Jesus as friend, we will create environments of worship and communion that support the discovery and use of each person's innate gifts, that nourish each soul and develop within each person the skills and confidence to succeed in life and ministry. Our understanding of evangelism is centered in it being the means through which the love of God is shared with the world. When such witness is done faithfully the church will be blessed through the diversity of our body and the breadth of our ideas and experiences.

Do not assume that such a declaration, which sounds virtuous and true, is easily achieved or without sometimes painful implications. It means we embrace the lives of people we may not understand, including choices with which we may not agree. It means we peer behind the surface of each one of us, knowing that if we believe in a God who creates human life, that God resides in the soul of every one. Our belief in community is founded upon our sure knowledge that the God in me seeks the God in you and that it is when we have encountered that divine reality at the very center of our faith that we finally, truly, know one another.

Reconciliation

Second, the path of the disciple calls us to reconciliation. We have for too long allowed separations to define us. We cannot proclaim ourselves to be a people committed to reconciliation when we have festering sores of division within our own community. We will identify and seek to repair breaches in relationships within our body and with those who share our witness of the Restoration movement, but for reasons of doctrinal conflict or personal conflicts have separated from us.

Tonight I extend an open invitation to those of the Restoration branches who are seeking a pathway to return. We desire to be reconciled. If we have hurt by our words or actions, we ask forgiveness. If we have been insufficiently patient or failed to understand, we will try to be better listeners. I extend the courtesies of my office, and those of other church leaders, to those who wish to dialogue with us about the ways we can share together from out of our common heritage. We pledge to be open, creative, and accepting and to seek every avenue of reconciliation.

We recognize that, in some cases, our differences over some issues may be such that we cannot return to full communion with each other. That does not indicate a failure to be reconciled if we are able to embrace one another in love, and extend God's blessing to each other, and share in such ways as may be satisfying. Judgments, characterizations, and attribution of unseemly motives are unworthy of our common callings to be disciples. Let us reason with one another, share the testimonies of our hearts, and be people of goodwill.

But our need to be reconciled extends beyond the boundaries of our own faith community. We have already begun and now must continue to overcome the things that separate us from other faiths and even from other religions of the world. Our commitment should be to coexist in love and peace, to be willing to learn from one another, to share our common witness to the extent we can, and to be respectful of those traditions that shape the souls of billions of people around the world.

To do so is not to divest ourselves of the zeal inherent in our own witness. It is to embrace the fundamental principle of the Christian, which is love of God and love of neighbor. For too long we have worried that exposure of our faith to those with differing beliefs somehow requires dilution of what we believe. To the contrary, a willingness to step forward aggressively into our communities, to sit at the table with priests and pastors, to engage in interfaith discussions, is a way of proclaiming to the world who we are. We have things to say, contributions to make, a wonderful story worth recounting. Let us be reconciled to brothers and sisters of other faiths and religions by authentically expressing our witness and being respectful of theirs.

Sharing

Third, the path of the disciple is to share willingly from the blessings of our lives. One of the cardinal principles of our faith is stewardship, but for too long we have shunted it off into its own box, left it to be interpreted by those with "temporal responsibilities," and wrongly assumed that it was about money and budgets. Tonight we join with the Presiding Bishopric in committing ourselves to a process of truly merging the function of the steward with the heart of the disciple.

Let's be blunt. Our people have been generous when challenged—witness the response to the building of the Temple and the call to support Transformation 2000. However, the overall interpretation of stewardship as we now understand it has increasingly lost the full support of several generations of church members. We continue to search for ways to define it so as to capture the imagination of each successive generation of stewards. We can no longer nod our head appreciatively about a principle, knowing all the while that many of us have not found a way to get it into our bone marrow. We *must* do something about it.

Our tithing filers and payers are the financial backbone of

the church. In 1996 the Order of Evangelists invited me and my family to come to a reception in recognition of my ordination as president of the church. My mother, then eighty years old, came along. Brother Graffeo provided my family members an opportunity to speak. He then asked Mom if she would like to say anything. Yeah, right, I thought. Like my soft-spoken, 5'1" mother is going to stand up in front of this group and give a speech!

"Well, I believe I do have a few words to say," she said. The blood drained from my face. Oh no, what on earth is she going to talk about? My mother stepped to the microphone—they were able to lower it that far. She then proceeded to lecture the Order of Evangelists on the importance of paying your tithing. She files her statement on January 1 each year, is annoyed that the Presiding Bishopric office is not open that day, and frets for hours if her calculations are off by twenty cents.

So what I am about to say is going to get me into a peck of trouble at Mom's house. But leadership requires courage that even means standing up

to your 5'1" mother. The way we are currently understanding the principle of tithing is no longer adequate to the needs of the church or the complex world in which we live. Don't misunderstand me. The principle of the tithe is a sound biblical concept absolutely essential to the well-being of the church. (Mom, now being resuscitated somewhere in the balcony, has just emitted a deep sigh of relief.)

But, friends, we urgently need a creative, scripturally sound, globally applicable theology of stewardship that lifts us beyond forms and formulas and gets us to the fundamental connection between the sharing of the tithe and the path of the disciple. A major assessment is already under way and some preliminary conclusions have been reached. We will engage the church in a dialogue about that over the coming months, and we invite all of you to join with us in that process.

Learning

Fourth, the path of the disciple requires us to be learners and teachers. Many of us live in a world of sound bytes, media imagery, and information that comes in very short bursts.

We have lost a sense of history. We settle for the superficial and the trite and call that knowledge. We let television networks and talk show hosts define our beliefs, want pamphlets instead of books, and declare resources to be without merit if they are not filled with pictures. I understand the importance of presentation, of design and visuals. But the disciple has to be concerned about content and meaning. We must get past the surface and invest ourselves deeply in the particulars of our faith so that we are not just willing disciples but competent ones as well.

To do so requires a careful reassessment of the Sunday school, which each year is becoming a weaker and weaker component of church life. A new vitality and energy must go into preparing ourselves for discipleship. If that requires a ravamping of the Sunday school format, so be it. If that requires having some people step forward and say "I'll do it!" then let's get off our haunches and get it done.

But more is required. Tonight I announce our intention to launch a five-year program, jointly engaged in by the World Church and local congregations, that has at its heart the imperative of making us a more scripturally literate people. To do so is to buck the trend of a culture where a dominant number of people seem to think Joan of Arc is married to Noah. Jay Leno's man-on-the-street interviews about biblical understandings depict the paucity of knowledge about even the basic Bible stories, things that once provided images and symbols common to all.

It is critically important that we continue to develop the Transformation 2000 objective of developing a theology of peace and justice "based on the scriptures, faith, and traditions of the Restoration movement." If we fail to do that work we will have simply created a call to social do-goodism that is without roots and devoid of the deeper call to embody the ministries of the Christ. To call the church to scriptural literacy is not at all to embrace a moribund fundamentalism that creates a life theology out of a handful of biblical quotations. To follow the road to a stifling literalism imprisons the scriptures in a cage and refuses to let them breathe and evolve as our lives listen to them in new ways.

Instead, we must develop a theology of scripture that appreciates the richness and depth of the sacred Word and points to the eternal truths that lurk behind its parables and stories and mythical abstractions. It is especially important for a church that claims more than one book of scripture and professes belief in continuing revelation to formulate a sound theology of the Word that allows room for God to speak through both ancient and contemporary forms.

We begin by committing ourselves to develop programs of scriptural literacy that train our children, build a foundation for our youth, deepen and enrich the understandings of adults, and assure all of us that what we do is founded on God's Word.

But even that is not enough to make us the trained disciples we are called to become. In a couple of days we will introduce a piece of legislation that asks the World Conference to approve the initial steps toward establishment of a seminary to train those who wish to engage in full-time ministry or to enhance their self-sustaining ministry in this faith community.

I grew up in congregations led by wonderful men who felt that preparation for worship was simply to let the Spirit work its wonders. My experience was that sometimes the Spirit made a miraculous appearance and sometimes it decided that today it would work with those who had prepared a bit more. Occasionally the Spirit has bailed me out when I wasn't ready, but it usually finds a pretty direct way of reminding me that being an effective witness may sometimes be about miracles but more often it is about preparation.

We have completed two years of study and discussion and believe we are ready to launch an initiative to establish a seminary for the benefit of the church. We intend to use partnerships with Graceland College and with other institutions of higher education to harness the amazing technologies of distance learning and Internet education, and utilize the broad skill base of talents we have among church members around the globe.

Spirituality

Fifth, the path of the disciple takes us to the mountaintop or into the forests or alongside the oceans in search of the God who resides within our own souls. The hunger for the spiritual is deep and abiding in what seems a profoundly secular world. It is the irony of our time that a generation often described as not religious is also described as *very* spiritual. The problem is that churches are seen as being about "beliefs" and somehow the spiritual quest has been uncoupled from that and connected with a smorgasbord of pursuits of the holy inspired by everything from Eastern mystics to massage therapies to spiritually centered exercise programs. I don't seek to ridicule or diminish those, many of which may have perfectly good value for adherents. What I do propose is that we get serious about the spiritual quest, recognize that there are many bruised and broken hearts in need of healing, and come to terms with the fact that a great many of those require new insights into the way the Spirit works among us.

I would say that the least developed of the three Transformation 2000 goals is healing of the spirit. It is the one thing that many of us would agree most needs to happen and perhaps the one thing we seem least able to get our arms around. It's time to push the limits a bit and to consider the ways we limit the Spirit by assuming the Spirit works only in certain ways. That Spirit has plunked me on the side of the head in some of the strangest situations and locations. I've argued with it a few times, declaring that it isn't supposed to show up *here*. And then the magic happens and I recognize that I was the one boxing it up and holding back its healing and redeeming touch.

Justice

Sixth, the path of the disciple requires us to stand up for justice. If we are to be faithful, we will become courageous witnesses of the call to stand for the dispossessed, to declare love where there is violence, to speak healing where there is estrangement, and to join with God in the journey toward the peaceable kingdom, where the unity of all creation is honored and celebrated.

When we speak of such things we usually think of the big issues of the world, of the struggle to overcome discriminations against people on the basis of race or creed, sexual orientation or gender, tribe or nationality. The question is joined at the point where power meets faith and where the dreams of our hearts are matched to the realities of our age.

But I want to suggest that justice-making is not just about those questions but also about the things we encounter every day in our congregations. David Schaal, the pastor of the Stone Church, has received permission from those involved so that I might share the following story. It may have some sensitive elements for them, but it is the real life of the church as it transforms the people whom it encounters.

April and Randy are teenage sister and brother. One year ago, they were living with their mother in a small Midwestern town. Without going into great personal detail, suffice it to say that their lives were very difficult and lacked the love, affirmation, and personal care that all of God's children deserve. In response to their circumstance they reacted in ways that reflected the frustration and loneliness of their hearts. Randy dropped out of high school; April left home and spent a year "on the street."

After a while, when their hearts' yearning for a place to call home intensified, they moved to Independence to live with their father and step-mother. In this new home they found safety, discipline, and love. Much to their surprise, they also found something else that would significantly change their lives. Their father and stepmother introduced them to a new group of friends—a youth group at the Stone Church.

In the fellowship of the senior high group, for the first time they found friends who cared for them, not for what they could get from them. Sensitive youth leaders listened to their stories, their concerns, their fears, and chatted with them about Jesus, about the church, and about how pleased they were that April and Randy had come to be a part of the group. Other Saints surrounded them with care and kindness. April is no longer on the street but in a home and a congregation where she and her brother are loved. Randy is back in school and working hard.

April was baptized about six weeks ago. Randy was baptized

two weeks later. Following one of the baptismal services, this delightful brother and sister embraced, and with broad smiles said to one another, "I can hardly believe how our lives have changed in just one year!"

Equally exciting is that both of them have voiced their desire to share their story with other teens and adults, hoping that their experience can be helpful to someone else. It is apparent that their lives are being transformed, because their concern is already being directed outward to others in need of their witness.

There is nothing extraordinary about this story, except for the fact that two lost kids were found, that a few ordinary folks joined together to demonstrate their love and care, and that this business of transformation isn't finally about numbers. It is about lives of people made whole because somebody had the courage to say: "This isn't fair. This isn't right. This isn't just."

These reflections about discipleship have pointed us toward community, reconciliation, sharing, learning, spirituality, and justice. I used to teach a lot of courses about the history of our movement, and it remains not only one of my loves but the fabric by which I understand the church. When I look at those concepts, they immediately connect to the ones I believe are deeply rooted in our history.

For community, we built cities in a search to blend the sacred and secular in a spatial environment. For reconciliation, we embraced the worth of persons, saying that all are called according to the gifts of God unto them. For sharing, we had all things in common and then evolved the principles of tithing and stewardship. For learning, we built a temple in Kirtland and called it a house of study, a house of prayer. For spirituality, we declared that God is not closed up in a box or a book, but that the Spirit wanders freely across the geography of our lives so as to find its way into our hearts. For justice, we endured the oppression and violence of the mobs and then adopted a church seal that placed the lion, the lamb, and the little child in a peaceful circle of love.

To be transformed is not to break faith with the past but to lay claim to a profoundly new continuity with the past. It is to discover in the seedbeds of our collective journey the nutrients that continue to provide us strength, hope, and vision. It is easier to reject the past than it is to restore its eternal truths in a new time. But it is to just such a radical form of discipleship that this beloved community of God's people is called.

We stand on the brink of a new era and at the end of an extraordinary journey through the twentieth century. Those decades took us from a church centered in the Midwestern United States, with a scattering of expressions in other parts of the Western world, to a people enriched by cultures and languages and lifestyles we would never have imagined even a half century ago. That has led us to search deeply within ourselves, to get in touch with what we really believe, and to venture in faith into the future. We are on the bridge and are prepared to set forth once again on a journey of discovery. Dare we say who we really are?

In 1994 the general officers of the church met in the mountains of Colorado to talk about faith and mission. We struggled and argued with one another and we did the things we do in meetings such as that—filling sheets of paper with all manner of markings and proposals. And then some amazing things began to happen among us. That Spirit of which we have been speaking appeared in our midst. There were tears and personal apologies for slights, some of them of short duration and others of longer time. There was a sense of unity that emerged around the mission statement we developed in the last full day of that week: "We proclaim Jesus Christ and promote communities of joy, hope, love, and peace." It seemed to capture it all.

And then, unexpected and unscheduled, discussion about the church's name emerged from out of the mission statement. Every person there can testify to what happened, to the sense of confirmation we felt that if we were to change our name we should declare ourselves to be the Community of Christ, blending our historic quest for community with the centrality of Jesus. In the closing worship, tears ran down our faces as we sang the hymn that Apostle McLaughlin wrote that night as the result of our discussion. It is called, "Community of Christ."

We did not promote the name. We shared it but did not try to sell it. We bore our testimony when asked, but most of us were meek, not wanting to be manipulative, wanting the church to come to a decision about this matter. By the next Conference in 1996 it was clear that the church was divided about evenly on the question.

As I began preparing for this Conference I found my mind turning again and again to how we present ourselves to the world. In the final analysis the world first meets us when we tell it our name. I surprised myself by finding how compellingly the question kept occurring in my mind. It had not been an issue on my agenda as I made my list of things we must address at this Conference, apart from recognizing that we had a resolution from the Florida Mission Center to consider. In a retreat setting with my counselors last February, in preparation for this Conference, I shared my thoughts with Bud and Ken and we talked together.

Just two weeks ago the World Church Leadership Council met in three days of sessions to explore the issues we face as Conference convenes, including many of the things I have spoken to already tonight. On the first day, we devoted an afternoon to a discussion of the church's name. It was a rational conversation. We were good at considering the pros and the cons. We had no consensus. We placed it on the agenda for the last afternoon of the council meeting, at a time when we would have completed our discussion of goals.

That afternoon began with prayer. Three of our number lifted up their voices to God that we might be led together to an understanding of the issue before us. And then began one of the truly blessed experiences of my life, and I dare say of the lives of all members of the council. We talked openly and honestly about our hopes and dreams for the church. We spoke of our childhoods and our nurturing by beloved Sunday school teachers and wonderful people who took us to youth camps and venerable church leaders whom we admired and wanted to emulate. Many of us had our eyes filled with tears because we all wanted so desperately for this church we love—with its amazing story of perseverance, inspiration, and sacrifice—to be continued to the generation of our children and their children.

The hearts of the council—many of them different persons than those who gathered in Colorado in 1994—again were blended together in an almost unanimous embrace of the desire to add to ourselves a new name that we may use to more adequately express our contemporary witness in the world, while retaining the beloved long name we have carried so long as the official, legal name of the church. The discussion was ended most poignantly by President Sheehy who said, "This is the final decision I will be involved in after thirty-two years as a member of this council. I can think of no more important issue to center on than the question of our identity. I will always be a member of the Reorganized Church of Jesus Christ of Latter Day Saints, but I want my children to be members of the Community of Christ."

Tonight I share with you my support for a new name to define our mission in a new time.

I stand with my colleagues on the World Church Leadership Council to bring leadership to this discussion and to bear our testimony of what has happened among us.

In a couple of days I will introduce legislation to substitute for that presented by the Florida Region. Our legislation will provide that we will make this change only when a two-thirds majority of the World Conference expresses its willingness to risk with us. If a change is approved, it will not be immediate. We will provide a time to develop a strategy for communication, to explore all legal issues, and to share more broadly with the church members who have not been the beneficiaries of our discussion.

It is a glorious time in the life of the church. We confess that we do not always live in the world we proclaim. We seek to be the best disciples we can be, and sometimes that means we will go outside our comfort zones to discover where the truth will lead us.

I return to the chambered nautilus, envisioned more than sixty years ago as the symbol for our Temple and then incorporated serendipitously into the architect's design. The poem by Oliver Wendell Holmes has a concluding verse. It was recited most often by the Temple Builders when they met. It reads:

Build thee more stately mansions,
   O my soul,
As the swift seasons roll!
Leave thy low-vaulted past!
Let each new temple, nobler than
   the last,
Shut thee from heaven with a
   dome more vast,
Till thou at length art free,
Leaving thine outgrown shell by
   life's unresting sea!

Let us venture forth, brothers and sisters, into the new day that the Lord has made. Let us together, as a community committed to the Christ, walk the path of the disciple, for only that path leads us from the limitations of our own minds to the expansive and marvelous frontiers God has promised to those who respond.

They were fishermen mostly, and they stood by "life's unresting sea." They became disciples in one mystical moment of transforming faith when they laid down their nets and lifted up their eyes, hearing for the first time the words of Jesus, who said only this: *"Follow me."*

Contributors

Ken Barrows—appointee minister assigned to First Canadian Mission Center, Calgary, Canada

Danny A. Belrose—presiding evangelist, World Church

Andrew Bolton—coordinator of Peace and Justice Ministries, World Church

Robert P. Bruch—retired appointee minister, Independence, Missouri

Darlene Caswell—adult ministries specialist (recently retired), World Church

Mary Jacks Dynes—appointee minister assigned to Pacific Northwest Region and president of seventy, Ridgefield, Washington

Jane Gardner—coordinator of Worship Ministries, World Church

Frank Kelley—appointee minister assigned to San Francisco Bay Stake, Fremont, California

Bob Kyser—senior president of seventy and missionary ministries coordinator, World Church

Gregg McDonald—bishop, Africa Region, World Church

Larry McGuire—appointee minister assigned to North Central States Region, Chicago, Illinois

Grant McMurray—prophet-president, World Church

Dave Nii—appointee minister assigned to Denver Stake and West Central States Region, Littleton, Colorado

Dave Schaal—appointee minister assigned to Central Field, as Tri-Stake Mission Center president, Independence, Missouri

Sherrie Taylor and Ray Taylor—Shreveport, Louisana

Joey Williams—executive youth minister, Tri-Stake Mission Center, Independence, Missouri

Notes

Notes

Notes